Unveiling
ANCIENT
BIBLICAL
SECRETS

Unveiling
ANCIENT
BIBLICAL
SECRETS

Larry HUCH

WHITAKER
HOUSE

UNVEILING ANCIENT BIBLICAL SECRETS:
Receiving the Miracles You Have Been Waiting For

Larry Huch Ministries
P.O. Box 610890
Dallas, TX 75261
www.LarryHuchMinistries.com / www.newbeginnings.org

ISBN: 978-1-60374-258-0
Printed in the United States of America
© 2011 by Larry Huch

Whitaker House
1030 Hunt Valley Circle
New Kensington, PA 15068

Library of Congress Cataloging-in-Publication Data

Huch, Larry.
 Unveiling ancient Biblical secrets : receiving the miracles you have been waiting for / Larry Huch.
    p. cm.
 Summary: "By understanding the Jewish roots of the Christian faith, believers can rediscover the destiny and blessing that God intends for His people"—Provided by publisher.
 ISBN 978-1-60374-258-0 (trade pbk. : alk. paper) 1. Blessing and cursing—Biblical teaching. 2. Covenants—Religious aspects—Biblical teaching. 3. Christian life—Biblical teaching. 4. Judaism (Christian theology) I. Title.
 BS680.B5H83 2011
 248.2—dc23
                    2011023323

1 2 3 4 5 6 7 8 9 10 11   ⑴ 18 17 16 15 14 13 12 11

Dedication

This book is dedicated to my children and their spouses, who share our passion and love for God, His Word, His people, and our ministry. You are all wonderful people and such an integral part of our ministry team. To our daughter Anna and her husband, Brandin; our son, Luke, and his wife, Jen; and our daughter Katie: your very lives validate my purpose and fill my life with joy.

To my "Grandsugars," Asher, Judah, and Aviva Shalom, who are the light and joy of my life.

And most of all, to my wife, Tiz, who, for more than thirty-five years, has been my inspiration, support, and love. You bring joy to everything I do.

Contents

Introduction

*Every teacher of the law who has been instructed about the
kingdom of heaven is like the owner of a house who brings
out of his storeroom new treasures as well as old.*

(Matthew 13:52 NIV)

Jewish tradition suggests that one cannot even begin to understand true wisdom concerning the things of God until he or she
reaches sixty years old. Since I recently turned sixty, I guess I am
now officially qualified to be considered wise—although I'm sure
there are some who would beg to differ! During my thirty-five years
as a Christian, I have been on a quest for God's wisdom and knowledge. As a pastor, I have sought the Lord and searched His Word for
the keys to unlock more of His anointing and miraculous power.

During this journey, I began to recognize a wide gap between
what God has promised in His Word and what actually manifests in
the lives of believers. If you have read my previous books, *Free at Last*
and *The Torah Blessing*, you know that my journey has led me to a
never-ending search of the ancient Jewish roots of our faith. I can
honestly tell you that this has been the most exciting journey of my
spiritual life. As I have intensely studied God's Word, He has revealed
incredible mysteries and released supernatural miracles! Tiz and I
have seen more and greater miracles in these last few years than in
all our previous years together. That is why I am so passionate about
what the Lord has been revealing to me. What God has done for me,
He is going to do for you! The miracles we have seen Him do in our
lives, and in the lives of others, He is about to do in your life, as well!

In the ancient Hebrew language, there is no equivalent for the
word *coincidence*. So, if you are reading this book, I believe that God

has led you to join me on this incredible journey. I need to inform you, however, that this is a never-ending journey! The more you begin to understand, the more you will hunger to know. The more you experience the manifestation of God's covenant promises, the more you will realize what you've been missing and what's available. And the more God does for you, the more you will want to see Him do for others, as well.

In the New Testament, Jesus said, *"Every teacher of the law who has been instructed about the kingdom of heaven is like the owner of a house who brings out of his storeroom new treasures as well as old."* Please keep that in mind as you read this book. We will be studying the Word of God through the eyes of a Jewish Messiah—from the perspective of the "old" and the "new." As these ancient biblical truths are unveiled, the miraculous will be unleashed into your life!

Let me show you an example of this in a Scripture that you are probably already familiar with. In Ecclesiastes 4, it says,

> *Two are better than one, because they have a good reward for their labor. For if they fall, one will lift up his companion. But woe to him who is alone when he falls, for he has no one to help him up. Again, if two lie down together, they will keep warm; but how can one be warm alone? Though one may be overpowered by another, two can withstand him. And a threefold cord is not quickly broken.* (verses 9–12)

Throughout most of this passage, Solomon, the author of Ecclesiastes, refers to two cords. From the Hebrew teaching, we know that these two cords represent the covenant between you and God. God is saying, in effect, "If you fall, I'll lift you up; if you're cold, I'll warm you; if you're hungry, I'll feed you." Then, in the last verse, he says, *"A threefold cord is not quickly broken."* In Hebrew, that third cord represents a teacher who is your friend. It's not enough just to have a covenant between you and God; you also need somebody to teach you. You need a friend to guide you.

One purpose of this book is for me to come alongside you, as a friend and a teacher, to guide you and to teach you the secrets of the covenant between you and God. So, for a little while, may I be your friend to guide you on this journey?

This book will not only have an impact on your personal perceptions of God's Word, but it will also have a tremendous impact on your personal life, family, finances, and future—not someday but now!

Perhaps you've heard of the prophecy that says when Jesus returns to Jerusalem, He is going to rebuild the tabernacle of David. Before God can build a physical tabernacle of David in Jerusalem, however, He's going to build the spiritual tabernacle of David in your heart and in your life.

There are three differences in the tabernacle of David that made it different from all other temples. First, the level of praise in the worship was supernatural and prophetic. It was inspired by God and released a supernatural anointing that transformed people's hearts and lives. Second, there was no Holy of Holies, and therefore no separation between God and man. Third, and this was most important, there was no middle wall that divided the Gentiles from the Jews. Everyone who served God, everyone who loved the God of Abraham, Isaac, and Jacob, studied and worshipped God together.

Another purpose of this book is to tear down that wall that divides Jew from Gentile. What will happen when we tear down that wall? The same thing that happened in the tabernacle of David! God walked among His people without separation, and signs and wonders followed. As you read this book, God will not only unveil His mysteries, but He will also come out from behind the veil and walk through your life, releasing signs, wonders, and miracles. Then, the unveiling of these ancient mysteries and truths will reveal the power and anointing of the Lord!

Let's rebuild the tabernacle of David in our hearts and usher in the rebuilding of the tabernacle of David in the world.

Get ready for the unveiling!

—Larry Huch

PART
I

Unveiling the Children
of Miracles

You Are Created for Greatness

Whoever runs after greatness, greatness will elude him; whoever flees from greatness, greatness will pursue him.
                                        —Hebrew Proverb

To some, God is great because He makes the wind blow. For others, His greatness has more to do with the fact that He created the entire universe—time and space, matter and energy—out of a void. But God is far beyond any of this. God is so great that He stoops down to listen to the prayers of a small child. He knits together fields and forests but also paints the petals of each flower. What a great God we serve! And you, my friend, are created in His image. (See Genesis 1:26–27.) Therefore, you are created for greatness!

When Tiz and I started our first church, in Santa Fe, New Mexico, we were full of passion, zeal, and excitement. We were seeing hundreds of teenagers come out of the gangs, give their lives to the Lord, and be set free from drugs, violence, and crime. In fact, in our three years of ministry in Santa Fe, we saw more than six thousand kids give their lives to the Lord! You may find it hard to believe that, only a few months after we started, something happened to me that nearly defeated me and drove me out of the ministry.

One Sunday morning, as I was preaching, a man walked into the church and stood in the back, staring at me. Then, he shook his head, turned around, and walked out. Over the next few weeks, the same thing happened during each service. Finally, I scheduled a guest speaker for one of our Wednesday night services. After I opened the service and turned it over to the speaker, I went to the back and stood by the door. Sure enough, a few minutes later, that same man walked into the service, stood there for a few minutes, and then walked out. I followed him into the parking lot and said, "Sir, excuse me, is there something I can help you with?"

He spun around and shouted, "You have no right! You have no right! You have no right to preach the gospel!" Then, he began to name things that I had done in my past—things that no one else knew. His words went straight to my heart. I stood there speechless as he stormed away. All the terrible things I had done in my past, before I met the Lord, began to flood my mind. A cloud of condemnation settled over my thoughts and emotions. I thought, *He's correct. I have no right to preach the gospel. I have done such horrible things; I have no right to stand in God's holy pulpit and preach His Word.*

In that moment, God spoke to me, saying, *Don't you ever let anyone bring up the sins of your past! Don't you ever let anyone condemn you about what I have washed clean! Don't you ever let anyone drive you out of what I have called you to do!*

With those words, God snapped me out of what the enemy was trying to do. From that moment, I have never looked back.

Listen. Satan is always going to bring up your past and throw condemnation on your life. That's why the Bible calls him *"the accuser of our brethren"* (Revelation 12:10). Those accusations are the most powerful and effective weapons he will use to try to defeat and destroy us. But, they will work only *if* we allow them to affect us. The Lord set me free from my past more than thirty years ago, and He will do the same for you today. *"If the Son makes you free, you shall be free indeed"* (John 8:36).

When the enemy accuses you of your past, you just remind him about his future!

As far as the east is from the west, so far has He removed our transgressions from us. (Psalm 103:12)

He will again have compassion on us, and will subdue our iniquities. You will cast all our sins into the depths of the sea. (Micah 7:19)

When God cleanses us from the sins of our past, He throws them into the deepest part of the sea. Then, He puts up a sign that says, "No Fishing!"

Renewing Your Mind

In order to fully overcome the sins of your past, however, you need to change the way you think. The Bible says, *"As [a man] thinks in his heart, so is he"* (Proverbs 23:7). Later, I will discuss the power of thought, but for now, let me begin with *"the renewing of your mind"* (Romans 12:2).

> **When God cleanses us from the sins of our past, He throws them into the deepest part of the sea.**

Deuteronomy 28 makes it clear that if we serve God and keep His commandments, we will be blessed beyond our wildest dreams.

And all these blessings shall come upon you and overtake you, because you obey the voice of the LORD your God: Blessed shall you be in the city, and blessed shall you be in the country. Blessed shall be the fruit of your body, the produce of your ground and the increase of your herds, the increase of your cattle and the offspring of your flocks. Blessed shall be your basket and your kneading bowl. Blessed shall you be when you come in, and blessed shall you be when you go out. (Deuteronomy 28:2–6)

But if we forsake God and reject His commandments, we open up our lives to all kinds of destruction.

> *But it shall come to pass, if you do not obey the voice of the LORD your God, to observe carefully all His commandments and His statutes which I command you today, that all these curses will come upon you and overtake you: Cursed shall you be in the city, and cursed shall you be in the country. Cursed shall be your basket and your kneading bowl. Cursed shall be the fruit of your body and the produce of your land, the increase of your cattle and the offspring of your flocks. Cursed shall you be when you come in, and cursed shall you be when you go out.* (Deuteronomy 28:15–19)

There is no need to fear this, however, because I have found that God makes it easy to be blessed. It's not a big mystery. He has laid out an easy-to-follow guide to all His blessings: His law. In fact, contrary to what many of you have probably heard, God's law is not about rules and regulations and legalism; it is about revealing a pathway to all of His blessings and goodness!

My purpose in revealing these truths to you is not so that we might all become biblical scholars. Rather, I want to unveil these ancient hidden truths so that God can release all of His miraculous power and blessings into your life! I know that each one of us wants to experience a happy, blessed, and prosperous life. What might surprise you is that, even more than you want that, God, our Father, wants it for us!

In Acts 8, we read an account of a discussion between the apostle Philip and an Ethiopian eunuch who was struggling with the book of Isaiah. Philip asked, *"Do you understand what you are reading?"* (verse 30). The eunuch replied, *"How can I, unless someone guides me?"* (verse 31). Later, in Luke, it is written that God *"opened* [the disciples'] *understanding, that they might comprehend the Scriptures"* (Luke 24:45).

Let me say it once more: the purpose of this book is for me to come alongside you, as a friend and a teacher, guiding you and revealing the secrets of the covenant between you and God.

I pray that God will open your mind and heart—as He has for me—that you will begin to understand the Scriptures, as well as His amazing love.

When I started serving God, I was told that He didn't care about our earthly lives as much as He cared about our future lives in heaven. He didn't care if I had a home or a car. The people who told me such things even went so far as to suggest that, in this life, God would "put you to the test" through various sicknesses, hardships, and calamities.

Then, when Tiz and I were pastoring a church in Australia, something happened that changed my life. I had a vision from God in which I saw a tremendous outpouring of His power and anointing. I saw God flooding His people with favor and blessings. This came as a shock to me because I had an image in my head of Him being an "angry God."

As I was having this vision, I was overwhelmed by God's love and goodness. I told Him, "I want to be a part of this. What do I have to do to be used by You to touch people this way?" I thought that God's response would be that I must suffer before I could see such things. But instead, this is what God said: *Tell My people that I'm a good God.* What a revelation! God is a *good* God. He's not a hard taskmaster. He's not mad or mean or angry.

Then, God brought Scriptures to my heart:

For the eyes of the LORD run to and fro throughout the whole earth, to show Himself strong on behalf of those whose heart is loyal to Him. (2 Chronicles 16:9)

It is your Father's good pleasure to give you the kingdom. (Luke 12:32)

Beloved, I pray that you may prosper in all things and be in health, just as your soul prospers. (3 John 1:2)

The rabbis teach us that God has created us for greatness. He didn't create us to fail. He didn't create us to be sick, poor, defeated, and suffering. As a matter of fact, God is so determined for us to walk in greatness that He's signed a contract with us in the blood of His own Son, Jesus. It's called a *covenant*.

Your Covenant with God

In our modern world, the word *covenant* doesn't have much meaning. A generation ago, you could do business with a handshake agreement. A person's word meant something. A person of honor was one who kept his word. Today, it is rare to take someone at his word. The modern business axiom is, "Get it on paper with a signature—in triplicate!"

The principle Tiz and I base our lives on is this: If God says it, He means it, and that settles it!

> *Men swear by someone greater than themselves, and the oath confirms what is said and puts an end to all argument. Because God wanted to make the unchanging nature of his purpose very clear to the heirs of what was promised, he confirmed it with an oath....It is impossible for God to lie....We have this hope as an anchor for the soul, firm and secure.*
>
> (Hebrews 6:16–19 NIV)

When God gives His word on something, you and I can count on it! It is impossible for Him to lie.

The Covenant Between You and God

Most Christians don't fully understand the word *covenant*. In fact, there's a secret that I want to show you.

Jesus taught about biblical covenants when He said,

> *This is My commandment, that you love one another as I have loved you. Greater love has no one than this, than to lay down one's life for his friends. You are My friends if you do whatever I command you. No longer do I call you servants, for a servant does not know*

what his master is doing; but I have called you friends, for all things that I heard from My Father I have made known to you. You did not choose Me, but I chose you and appointed you that you should go and bear fruit, and that your fruit should remain, that whatever you ask the Father in My name He may give you.
(John 15:12–16)

It's important to realize that Jesus said He was speaking what He had heard from the Father. Here, Jesus gave us five powerful points that characterize a covenant between two people—in this case, you and God. First, this covenant is made because Jesus loves you. *"This is My commandment, that you love one another as I have loved you."* Second, Jesus loves you so much, He was willing to die for you. *"Greater love has no one than this, than to lay down one's life for his friends."* Third, He doesn't look down on you as someone who is unworthy. *"No longer do I call you servants,…but I have called you friends."* Fourth, because of this covenant of love, Jesus will hold nothing back from you. *"All things that I heard from My Father I have made known to you."* Fifth, because of this covenant, you will reap a harvest of blessing, joy, peace, prosperity, health, and happiness. *"That you should go and bear fruit, and that your fruit should remain, that whatever you ask the Father in My name He may give you."*

The Covenant Between David and Jonathan

One of the greatest examples of covenant in the Bible is the one that was made between David and Jonathan. Let's see how that pattern of covenant mirrors God's covenant with us. It is a covenant between David, a no-name shepherd boy, and Jonathan, the son of a king.

The soul of Jonathan was knit to the soul of David, and Jonathan loved him as his own soul. Saul took him that day, and would not let him go home to his father's house anymore. Then Jonathan and David

made a covenant, because he loved him as his own
soul. And Jonathan took off the robe that was on him
and gave it to David, with his armor, even to his sword
and his bow and his belt. So David went out wherever
Saul sent him, and behaved wisely. And Saul set him
over the men of war, and he was accepted in the sight
of all the people and also in the sight of Saul's ser-
vants.   (1 Samuel 18:1–5)

The first, and most important, thing we see is that
Jonathan made a covenant with David for one reason: he loved
him. *"The soul of Jonathan was knit to the soul of David, and*
Jonathan loved him as his own soul." Jonathan loved David as
he did his own soul.

David was a poor shepherd boy. When the prophet Samuel
came to see Jesse, David's father, to anoint one of his sons to
be the next king, Jesse never even considered David as a can-
didate.

And the Lord *said, "…Then invite Jesse to the sacri-*
fice, and I will show you what you shall do; you shall
anoint for Me the one I name to you." So Samuel did
what the Lord *said, and went to Bethlehem. And the*
elders of the town trembled at his coming, and said,
"Do you come peaceably?" And he said, "Peaceably;
I have come to sacrifice to the Lord. *Sanctify your-*
selves, and come with me to the sacrifice." Then he
consecrated Jesse and his sons, and invited them
to the sacrifice. So it was, when they came, that he
looked at Eliab and said, "Surely the Lord's anointed
is before Him." But the Lord *said to Samuel, "Do not*
look at his appearance or at the height of his stature,
because I have refused him. For the Lord does not see
as man sees; for man looks at the outward appear-
ance, but the Lord *looks at the heart." So Jesse called*

Abinadab, and made him pass before Samuel. And he said, "Neither has the LORD chosen this one." Then Jesse made Shammah pass by. And he said, "Neither has the LORD chosen this one." Thus Jesse made seven of his sons pass before Samuel. And Samuel said to Jesse, "The LORD has not chosen these."

(1 Samuel 16:2 10)

God did not pick any of the seven sons Jesse had brought before Samuel. Then, Samuel said,

"Are all the young men here?" Then [Jesse] *said, "There remains yet the youngest, and there he is, keeping the sheep."*

(verse 11)

We may never understand why Jesse didn't think to bring David in. For some reason, he never considered that God could possibly use somebody like David. I'd like to give Jesse the benefit of the doubt by assuming that David was far away, up in the mountains, tending his father's sheep. But,

> **You and I are not qualified in God's eyes because of who we are but because of who He is!**

sadly, that wasn't the case. Jesse said, *"There he is, keeping the sheep."* David was within sight, and yet his father didn't consider him to be a possibility. That's what the devil says to many of you. "God would never use you, bless you, or anoint you. You are not the tallest, fastest, or strongest. Why would God ever choose you?"

You need to understand something: you and I are not qualified in God's eyes because of who *we* are but because of who *He* is!

To be in *covenant* means being *permanently identified* with another party, maintaining *total loyalty* to a relationship that is *more sacred than life itself,* and *counting the cost* of how this agreement will affect your life.

1. Permanently Identified

Look again at 1 Samuel 18:3: *"Then Jonathan and David made a covenant."* In Hebrew, this verse is somewhat different. In Hebrew tradition, you don't sign a covenant; you *cut* a covenant. When David and Jonathan cut covenant, they each physically cut the palms of their hands with a knife. After the slices had been made, they would have rubbed ash from a fire into the wounds. As the scars healed, their darkened tissue made the men permanently identified with each other. No matter what happened in the future, those scars were evidence that these two men were permanently identified with and bonded to each other.

Similarly, the nail scars in Jesus' hands are a visible reminder that He is in permanent covenant with us. As we receive Jesus, we are reminded that we are permanently identified with Him. God told us that *"there is a friend who sticks closer than a brother"* (Proverbs 18:24). In John 3:16, Jesus told us of the lengths God would go to be in covenant with us: *"For God so loved the world that He gave His only begotten Son."* If our God and Savior sacrificed so much to make a deep covenant with us, it's only right that we should keep our part of the covenant. Let us not be ashamed of the gospel of Jesus Christ. Wherever we go, let's tell people that the kingdom of heaven is at hand. Let's share and demonstrate God's incredible love, wherever we go, to whomever we meet!

2. Total Loyalty

Even at the risk of going against his own father, Jonathan was loyal to David. Likewise, God is completely loyal to us.

The LORD your God, He is the One who goes with you. He will not leave you nor forsake you.
(Deuteronomy 31:6)

For He Himself has said, "I will never leave you nor forsake you."
(Hebrews 13:5)

In return, we are to be totally loyal to Jesus. We must commit to serve the Lord with all our hearts, with all our might, and with all our souls.

3. More Sacred Than Life Itself

In making a covenant with David, Jonathan was willing to risk his own life to save David's. In His covenant with us, Jesus sacrificed everything for us. His life was not taken from Him; He laid it down for us. *"By this we know love, because [Jesus] laid down His life for us. And we also ought to lay down our lives for the brethren"* (1 John 3:16).

4. Counting the Cost

Jonathan knew that being loyal to David it would cost him his kingdom. Jesus, while remaining loyal to the cause, counted the cost when He prayed, *"Father, if it is Your will, take this cup away from Me; nevertheless not My will, but Yours, be done"* (Luke 22:42). Being God, Jesus knew what it was going to cost Him to establish a covenant with us. He knew about the beatings and floggings and torture that lay ahead, yet, He said, in effect, "I'm willing to count the cost. Not My will but God's will be done." For us to count the cost, we need to be willing to *"go into all the world and preach the gospel to every creature"* (Mark 16:15).

Why would almighty God enter into covenant with *you*? For the same reason that Jonathan went into covenant with David: he loved him. Jonathan was rich and powerful; David was a shepherd boy. David had no money or power and knew no important people. David had nothing to offer the son of a king. Why, then, would Jonathan make a covenant with a "nobody"? Again, because he loved him. Listen to what Jesus calls you and me in the following passage:

> *Greater love has no one than this, than to lay down one's life for his friends....No longer do I call you servants,...but I have called you friends.* (John 15:13, 15)

Our friends are the people we like to spend time with. Maybe you and your friends enjoy going out to dinner, seeing movies, or attending ball games together. But in the time of Jesus, as well as in the time of David and Jonathan, a friend was more than that. In Hebrew tradition, a friend is someone I am committed to, someone for whom I will do everything in my power to protect. It is a person whom I will make sure is successful in everything he does.

> **God is committed to you. He is dedicated to seeing you succeed in every area of your life—in your home, marriage, family, finances, and health.**

This is what Jesus was saying to you. You are not a "nobody." You are not out there on your own. Don't listen to what the devil tells you. Why did Jesus come? *"For God so loved the world that He gave His only begotten Son..."* (John 3:16). Jesus came because God loves you. Then Jesus reminds us, *"No longer do I call you servants,...but I have called you friends."* Through Jesus, you are no longer just a shepherd boy, herding sheep in the desert. Now, you are a friend and covenant partner with God. Now, God is committed to you. He is dedicated to seeing you succeed in every area of your life—in your home, marriage, family, finances, and health.

Just as David didn't have much to offer Jonathan, you and I have even less to offer Jesus, the Son of God. So, why would God make this covenant of success with you and me? For the same reason that Jonathan did with David: He loves us!

Covenant Success

Let's take a closer look at the covenant made between David and Jonathan.

Clothed with Authority

One of the first things that happened was that *"Jonathan took off the robe that was on him and gave it to David"*

(1 Samuel 18:4). Imagine the clothes that David, a shepherd boy, must a have been wearing. They were most likely dirty and smelly from his living outside and working every day with sheep, worn and tattered from use. And, since David had just killed Goliath, they would have been soiled with sweat and the blood of the unclean Philistine. In one moment of time, David's filthy, defiled clothing was exchanged for the robe of royalty. Then, according to verse 5, *"wherever Saul sent him,...[David] was accepted in the sight of all the people and also in the sight of Saul's servants."* When Jonathan put the robe of royalty on David's shoulders, it wasn't just for show; it was a sign of authority. David may have been just a shepherd boy, someone who was even overlooked by his own father, but the moment Jonathan made a covenant with him and put the robe of royalty on him, everything changed. Jonathan was saying to the world, in effect, "Listen to whatever David says. From now on, when he speaks, he speaks for my kingdom!"

This is what Jesus has done for you and me. One of the devil's favorite tricks is to cause you confusion as to your identity. Like David, you and I came to God in rags. But, also like David, we have been stripped of those filthy rags and clothed in righteousness. *"Though your sins are like scarlet, they shall be as white as snow; though they are red like crimson, they shall be as wool"* (Isaiah 1:18). The apostle Paul wrote, *"And if [we are] children, then heirs; heirs of God and joint heirs with Christ, if indeed we suffer with Him, that we may also be glorified together"* (Romans 8:17).

Let me ask you a question: Are you a child of God? If your answer is yes, then the rest of what Paul said in the above verse is true. You are an heir, a joint heir, with Christ Jesus. This is exactly what took place between David and Jonathan. This is what Jesus is saying to you: "You are no longer a servant but a friend. My power is your power; My authority is your authority." David received authority from Jonathan, and all the people of the kingdom recognized it. Even the officers in Saul's kingdom saw the authority David now had. It's important that you understand the authority you have through the covenant with Jesus.

How do you pray? Here is how most people pray: "Lord Jesus, I ask You to get me a job." "Lord Jesus, I ask You to heal my body." "Lord Jesus, I ask You to get my child off drugs." If you pray this way, it is the number one reason you don't see your prayers answered. If we are asking Jesus for healing or blessing or deliverance, we are asking Him to do something He has already done. When Jesus died on the cross, He said, for all the world to hear, "It is finished!" (John 19:30). He has already done it for you. Now, He wants you to take off your servant rags and replace them with the robe of authority.

You Have the Keys!

Look at what Jesus said to Peter in Matthew:

> *And I will give you the keys of the kingdom of heaven, and whatever you bind on earth will be bound in heaven, and whatever you loose on earth will be loosed in heaven.* (Matthew 16:19)

Jesus didn't merely die for our sins, but He also reconnected us to every promise of God by the shedding of His blood.

Jesus was talking about keys. Keys are a symbol of authority. When someone has the keys, he has the power, or authority, to open doors, start engines, or unlock gates. Whoever has the keys has the power and the authority.

Before time began, only God had the authority. But in the book of Genesis, God created mankind and gave them—us—the keys, or the authority. After Adam and Eve sinned, those keys were passed on to the devil. Mankind, through disobedience to God, lost his authority—and the devil has been pulling our strings ever since.

Then came Jesus. Jesus obeyed God in the garden of Gethsemane, saying, *"Father, if it is Your will, take this cup away from Me; nevertheless not My will, but Yours, be done"* (Luke 22:42). The journey to Calvary had begun. Jesus didn't merely die for our sins, but He also reconnected us to every promise of God by the shedding of His blood. After Jesus died, and while His physical body was sealed in the tomb, His spirit went to the gates of Hades, where He defeated the devil and retrieved the keys of authority. *"I am He who lives, and was dead, and behold, I am alive forevermore. Amen. And I have the keys of Hades and of Death"* (Revelation 1:18).

Then, look again at Jesus' statement to Peter: *"I will give **you** the keys of the kingdom of heaven, and whatever **you** bind on earth will be bound in heaven, and whatever **you** loose on earth will be loosed in heaven"* (emphasis added). Just as Jonathan, through a covenant, gave David authority, Jesus has given you and me authority. Because of their covenant, David had the authority of the king behind him. You and I have the authority, not of just any king, but of the King of Kings.

You say, "Lord, my children are on drugs. Please remove drugs from their lives." Jesus says, "Don't you understand? I gave you the keys. Whatever you bind will be bound. Whatever you rebuke will be rebuked."

Can you imagine what would happen if all believers understood the authority we have in Jesus' name? David realized the authority he had through the covenant with Jonathan, and everyone else realized it, as well. Now is your time. Whatever you bind, the kingdom of God will back you up. Whatever you loose, God's kingdom will back you up. It's time to put on *"the garment of praise for the spirit of heaviness"* (Isaiah 61:3). Take off the garment of poverty; put on the King's robe of prosperity. Take off the garment of failure; put on the robe of success. From now on, when the devil says, "Who do you think you are?" tell him, "I am a friend, a covenant partner, and joint heir with Christ Jesus!"

Armed with Power

The second part of the covenant of success is also found in 1 Samuel 18:4: *"And Jonathan took off the robe that was on him and gave it to David, with his armor, even to his sword and his bow and his belt."* When Jonathan gave David his weapons, he was making a powerful statement. From that day forward, Jonathan's army was David's army; Jonathan's strength was David's strength. Whatever David said or did was to be given the same weight as if it had been said and done by the king himself. Jonathan was telling David, "From now on, you're not on your own." However, Jonathan knew that, even with the authority and backing of a king, David would still face battles and needed to be armed and ready.

Similarly, even though you have the power and authority of almighty God at your disposal, you will still face spiritual attacks from the evil one. Having faith does not exempt you from fighting battles; it is knowing that, no matter what battles you face, you will emerge victorious.

The apostle Paul said that we have God-given weapons at our disposal that are powerful and supernatural.

> *For though we walk in the flesh, we do not war according to the flesh. For the weapons of our warfare are not carnal but mighty in God for pulling down strongholds.* (2 Corinthians 10:3–4)

David faced Goliath with a slingshot and five smooth stones, but God gave him a supernatural victory over his enemy. When Jonathan put his belt and sword on David, however, God was increasing David's ability to win even greater victories.

In the chapters to come, I don't want to take away from the victories you have already won, but to multiply them. God wants to add to your arsenal of supernatural weapons. Was there a secret weapon in use when the woman who suffered from bleeding touched the hem of Jesus' garment and experienced healing?

(See Matthew 9:20–22.) Was there a supernatural weapon in use when God told the children of Israel to take His Word and put it on the doorposts of their homes? (See Deuteronomy 6:9.) The truth you understand will set you free.

Cutting Covenant

Earlier, I explained how David and Johnathan "cut" a covenant together by physically cutting the palms of their hands. In the Old Testament, when two men entered into covenant, a shedding of blood was required. There were two acts of bloodshed necessary.

First, there had to be a living sacrifice between the two people making covenant. Of course, we know Jesus was that living sacrifice between God and man. But there was a second way that blood was shed as a constant reminder to each man of his covenant agreement. As I explained earlier, when two men entered into a covenant with each other, they would take a knife or sword blade and cut the palms of their hands. Doing this resulted in dark scars that stood out from the rest of the skin on the hand.

When Jesus saw Thomas, He showed him the scars in the palms of His hands. (See John 20:25, 27.) In doing so, Jesus was saying, "I will never leave or forsake you." (See Hebrews 13:5.) When David and Jonathan "cut" covenant, Jonathan was saying, "David, your enemy will be my enemy, my army will be your army, and my kingdom will be your kingdom."

Just as Jonathan "cut covenant" with David, Jesus also cut covenant with you and me. When those Roman soldiers drove nails into the palms of Jesus' hands, His blood was shed to form a covenant with us.

Why does God ask us to lift up our hands? I believe that one reason is because it reminds us of that covenant. God is saying, "It may feel like you're alone, it may look like the enemy has you outnumbered, but you're not alone. I am with you."

Likewise, every time you lift up your hands, you are saying, "Devil, do you see my hands? These are covenant hands. I may look like I'm by myself, but I'm not. I have an army of angels behind me. The army of God is fighting for me."

At the beginning of this chapter, I told you a story about the condemnation I experienced as a new pastor. I felt so unworthy and unqualified. I told you of the man who came to me and said, "Who do you think you are? You have no right to preach the gospel!"

For a moment, I let his words get inside and take hold of my heart. In that moment, feelings of unworthiness and condemnation nearly robbed me of my future, my destiny, and all that God had for me. But, in the next moment, the Lord freed me from the guilt of my past and set me on an amazing course for my future. That's exactly what He wants to do for you today!

> **God created you for a purpose! You were not born to be a loser; you were born to be a winner!**

The enemy will tell you the same thing that he told me. He will try to condemn you and convince you that you aren't worthy of the blessings of God. He will ask, "Who do you think you are?"

Don't let anyone hold your past against you! The blood of Jesus has set you free from all the bondage and guilt! *"If God is for us, who can be against us?"* (Romans 8:31). When you were born, God created you for a purpose! You were not born to be a loser; you were born to be a winner! You were not born to be average; you were born for greatness! God, your Father, made a covenant of greatness with Abram, soon to be Abraham, the father of our faith. That covenant was not only for Abraham thousands of years ago. Jesus, our Messiah, confirmed that it is for you and me, today. When God makes a covenant and gives His word, we can count on it!

Now listen to this! In Isaiah, it says,

> *Can a woman forget her nursing child, and not have compassion on the son of her womb? Surely they may forget, yet I will not forget you. See, I have inscribed you on the palms of My hands; your walls are continually before Me.* (Isaiah 49:15–16)

This Scripture says that God is closer to us than a mother is to her child. Mother and child may eventually forget each other, but God says that He will never forget you, because the covenant He has made with you is inscribed on the palms of His hands. God the Father has your name inscribed on His hands! That's how much He loves you, personally! Yes, He loves the whole world, but He also loves you, individually.

God will never forget the covenant He has made with you. How could He? Your name is written on the palms of His hands! And, in these last days, God is opening our eyes so that we can become the children of miracles.

The Children of Miracles

*And it shall come to pass in the last days, says God,
that I will pour out of My Spirit on all flesh; your sons
and your daughters shall prophesy, your young men
shall see visions, your old men shall dream dreams.*

(Acts 2:17)

I f you are reading this book, I believe that God, in these last days, has handpicked you to be a chosen vessel for the fulfillment of prophecy. God is saying, in effect, "In these last days, *'I will pour out of My Spirit'* (Acts 2:17)." He is promising you that, as it pertains to all of His children, *"though your beginning was small, yet your latter end would increase abundantly"* (Job 8:7). There will be signs and wonders. There will be an end-time transfer of riches when *"the wealth of the sinner is stored up for the righteous"* (Proverbs 13:22).

You may be thinking, *Larry, I know that this is what the Bible says, but how do I know that it is for me?* There is a great rabbi who, in one of his last speeches, prophesied that the Messiah is ready to come. This means that both the Jew *and* the Gentile now believe that the Messiah is ready to come. Whether you think it will be His first coming or His second coming (I will address this in a later chapter), we can all agree on two things: (1) He is coming soon, and (2) He is coming to Israel and to Jerusalem.

That famous rabbi went on to say that the Messiah is ready to come, but, first, something else will happen: there will be a group of Gentiles (non-Jews) *whose eyes will be opened* in order to understand Jewish teachings such as Passover, Shabbat, Rosh Hashanah, and Yom Kippur. At first, those around them will think it strange, but then, these Gentiles will begin to see such miracles and blessings of God in a way that draws the attention of the entire world. Those whose eyes will be opened will be called "the children of miracles."

Now, you are probably thinking, *If this is true, why haven't I heard it before?* You have. In Christianity, many of us refer to it as "the Latter Rain," a time when God will hold nothing back. It will be a time when He captures the attention of the whole world through signs, wonders, and miracles. According to ancient Jewish teaching, "No one is smart enough to teach these 'mysteries of the Bible,' and no one is smart enough to understand them." Therefore, if God is showing you these teachings—remember, there is no Hebrew equivalent for *coincidence*—it is because He has handpicked you to be a "child of miracles" in these last days. It is because He wants to use you to get the world's attention, just as God said in Malachi 3:12: *"All nations will call you blessed."* Or, as He stated in His covenant with Abraham (Abram, at the time), *"In you all the families of the earth shall be blessed"* (Genesis 12:3). Not only is God going to do great miracles *for* you; He also is going to do great miracles *through* you! You are an intricate part of the "latter rain" outpouring of God's Spirit, revelation, anointing, signs, and wonders, as well as His end-time transfer of wealth! You and I are stepping into end-time destiny!

> **Not only is God going to do great miracles *for* you, He also is going to do great miracles *through* you!**

Changing the Way You Think

Before I go any further, let's look at a couple of Scriptures.

O LORD, my strength and my fortress, my refuge in the day of affliction, the Gentiles shall come to You from the ends of the earth and say, "Surely our fathers have inherited lies, worthlessness and unprofitable things." Will a man make gods for himself, which are not gods? "Therefore behold, I will this once cause them to know, I will cause them to know My hand and My might; and they shall know that My name is the LORD." (Jeremiah 16:19–21)

Through the generations, God has come to His people in order to do as the prophet Elisha asked: *"LORD, open the eyes of these men, that they may see"* (2 Kings 6:20).

That is exactly what God is going to do for you through this book. He is going to open your eyes to the truth of His power, hidden within His Word. He is going to open your eyes to the power of His might that surrounds you. He is going to open your eyes and show you how to use *"the weapons of our warfare"* (2 Corinthians 10:4). He is going to open your eyes in these last days so you can walk in the reality of what the apostle John taught us: *"He who is in you is greater than he who is in the world"* (1 John 4:4).

Perhaps now you are thinking, *Larry, can God really open my spiritual eyes? Are there really mysteries in the Bible that I haven't seen yet?* Don't worry. Throughout the Bible, there are examples of God opening the eyes of His people to experience a deeper revelation of the spiritual realm.

Open my eyes, that I may see wondrous things from Your law. (Psalm 119:18)

I have chosen the way of truth; I have set my heart on your laws. I hold fast to your statutes, O LORD; do not let me be put to shame. I run in the path of your commands, for you have set my heart free.

(verses 30–32 NIV)

The apostle Paul was aware of the difference between a "baby Christian" and a mature believer. *"When I was a child, I spoke as a child, I understood as a child, I thought as a*

child; but when I became a man, I put away childish things"
(1 Corinthians 13:11). When we are babies in the faith, God
gives us the milk of His Word. But, as we grow and mature, we
are able to digest meatier concepts. (See Hebrews 5:12–14.) To
me, the most exciting thing is that God's Word is a never-ending
journey of unveiled mysteries! As a Christian for over thirty-five
years, I can honestly say that I am more excited now about the
things of God than I have ever been! Tiz and I are beginning to
see the types of outpourings of the Spirit that we had only read
about. And the more we learn and understand God's Word, the
more the blessings and miracles are released into our lives!

For the first fifteen years of our Christian lives, Tiz and I
were taught that God does not care as much about what happens to us in this life as He does about the world to come.
Thus, according to this mind-set, God didn't care whether or
not we drove a nice car or lived in a beautiful home. We were
taught that it was wrong to desire such things because they
were worldly. Eventually, we discovered the truth: God *does*
want to bless us here in this world, and Jesus came to give
us an abundant life on earth. Jesus said, *"I have come that
they may have life, and that they may have it more abundantly"*
(John 10:10). One key to experiencing abundant life is changing the way you think.

During a recent celebration of Pentecost, our church had
invited one of the world's foremost collectors of ancient Bibles
and Torah scrolls to be interviewed at our service. During the
interview, he showed us several stunning artifacts that provided incredible insights into why returning to our Jewish roots
is so important. The first artifacts were the earliest pages of
the New Testament that have been discovered to date. They
were not written in Greek but in western Aramaic, the language spoken by the Jewish people at that time. Looking at
these ancient pages of the Bible proved to me once again that
studying the Word of God with a Hebrew mind-set, as opposed
to a Western, Greco-Roman mind-set, is the key to our miracle

breakthrough. There are mysteries and secrets that will be unveiled only when we are able to study Scripture the way it was written in the beginning.

The other artifact the collector showed us was an ancient Geneva Bible from the 1500s that was used as one of the references for translating Scripture into what is known today as the King James Version. This particular Bible is valued at over one million dollars because it was the actual one used by the translators. It was stunning to see the Scripture passages that had been crossed out and replaced with new definitions. This served as a reminder that when you are working from a translation and not the text in its original language, you are reading Scripture that has been shaped, in part, by the translators.

The Seed and the Soil

I want you to look at a powerful teaching of Jesus from Matthew 13. This teaching is more for you and me today than ever before. It's a revelation that assures us that our latter houses will be greater than the former houses. (See Haggai 2:9.)

Behold, a sower went out to sow. And as he sowed, some seed fell by the wayside; and the birds came and devoured them. Some fell on stony places, where they did not have much earth; and they immediately sprang up because they had no depth of earth. But when the sun was up they were scorched, and because they had no root they withered away. And some fell among thorns, and the thorns sprang up and choked them. But others fell on good ground and yielded a crop: some a hundredfold, some sixty, some thirty. He who has ears to hear, let him hear! (Matthew 13:3–9)

Jesus was teaching about the seed, which is God's Word. He was also teaching about the soil, which is mankind or anyone who hears the Word. The seed is perfect; there is nothing wrong with God's Word. It is given in order to produce a "*hundredfold*" blessing. The seed always brings forth abundance, favor, health, and blessings in our lives—the soil. It is always able to do "*exceedingly abundantly above all that we ask or think*" (Ephesians 3:20).

Thus, the question is, why doesn't it? Why is it that we see only *some* blessed, *some* healed, *some* prosperous, and *some* whose debts are canceled? God doesn't want His blessings to rest only on *some*; He wants them to rest on all of His creation. He wants them to rest on you!

Here is the secret: first, Jesus taught that some people are simply bad soil. In such cases, the seed is perfect, but the soil is bad. Other seed went by the wayside and was stolen by birds in the same way that the world and its ways can devour us. Some seed fell on stony ground and dried up because it had no depth for its roots. It gave up too soon. Some seed fell among thorns that choked them out. Remember, in the garden of Eden, the land had nothing but the blessing of God on it. There was no sickness, no poverty, no anger, and no addictions. But after Adam disobeyed God, he and Eve were cast out of the garden. The Bible says that God cursed the land with "*thorns and thistles*" (Genesis 3:18). Therefore, the thorns Jesus was talking about were curses that can kill the harvest God has for you.

> God doesn't want His blessings to rest only on some; He wants them to rest on all of His creation.

Most of us are able to understand the first three types of soil that Jesus was talking about—the wayside, the stony soil, and the thorny soil. But what about the fourth type of soil? This is the *good* soil, which is made up of all who believe in the Lord. If Jesus was talking about good soil that is ready for the harvest, why did He say it will yield "*a crop: some a hundredfold, some sixty, some thirty*"? You are good soil. In these last days, I believe that God wants you to be that "*hundredfold*" child of

God—a child of miracles. Why the variance? Why, for those of us who are "good soil," do some get thirty-, some sixty-, and some a hundredfold? Why don't we all get one hundredfold?

Look at Matthew 13:9: *"He who has ears to hear, let him hear!"* When the Lord mentions *"ears"* and our ability to *"hear,"* He is saying something important. Beyond just our physical ears and their ability to comprehend language and sounds, He is also talking about our spiritual understanding.

> *They have ears, but they do not hear.* (Psalm 115:6)

> *Having eyes, do you not see? And having ears, do you not hear? And do you not remember?* (Mark 8:18)

There are people who can hear and see physically, yet, spiritually, they don't "see" it; they don't understand. Now, let's look at how Jesus explained His parable of the seed:

> *For whoever has, to him more will be given, and he will have abundance; but whoever does not have, even what he has will be taken away from him.*
> (Matthew 13:12)

You might read this and think, *Boy, that doesn't seem fair.* It seems like the biblical version of "the rich get richer and the poor get poorer." But let's read it in context. Jesus was not referring to physical things but to spiritual things. He was talking about the wisdom of God's Word. Look at verse 11: *"Because it has been given to you to know the mysteries of the kingdom of heaven, but to them it has not been given."* Jesus wants you and me to know—to hear and to understand—the mysteries of the kingdom.

> *But we speak the wisdom of God in a mystery, the hidden wisdom which God ordained before the ages for our glory.* (1 Corinthians 2:7)

> *For he who speaks in a tongue does not speak to men but to God, for no one understands him; however, in the spirit he speaks mysteries.* (1 Corinthians 14:2)

In Him we have redemption through His blood, the for-
giveness of sins, according to the riches of His grace
which He made to abound toward us in all wisdom
and prudence, having made known to us the mystery
of His will, according to His good pleasure which He
purposed in Himself, that in the dispensation of the
fullness of the times He might gather together in one all
things in Christ, both which are in heaven and which
are on earth; in Him. (Ephesians 1:7–10)

This is a great mystery, but I speak concerning Christ
and the church. (Ephesians 5:32)

I want to share with you how, after many years as a
Christian and a pastor, I had my eyes opened by the Lord to the
mysteries—the secrets of God's Word—as never before. Don't
get me wrong; my life serving God had been wonderful. But,
to be honest, thirtyfold is fine; sixtyfold is better, more than I
deserve; but I desire all the blessings of God. I desire to reap
one hundredfold. If we allow Him to open our eyes, according
to Matthew 13:12, the more wisdom we have, the more He will
give us. Think about that. If we allow it, He will give us more
wisdom, then more, and then even more.

Why is this so important? God told us, *"My people are*
destroyed for lack of knowledge" (Hosea 4:6). By saying, **"My**
people," He was not referring to the ungodly who reject God's
Word, but to those who believe in Him, serve Him, pray to Him,
and trust Him. The devil of poverty, debt, depression, addiction,
and divorce can destroy the people of God for only one reason:
"lack of knowledge."

Then Jesus said to those Jews who believed Him, "If
you abide in My word, you are My disciples indeed.
And you shall know the truth, and the truth shall
make you free." (John 8:31–32)

How many times have you heard people say, "Jesus said,
'The truth will make you free'"? I used to say it all the time.

But that's not what the verse says. Look again. *"And you shall know the truth, and the truth shall make you free."* When we "know" the truth—when we understand it—*then*, that truth, which we finally understand after our eyes have been opened, will become alive in every area of our lives and set us free—free from poverty, free from debt, free from sickness, and free from anger. The church, without spot or blemish, will become His glorious bride.

Proverbs tells us, *"Wisdom is the principal thing; therefore get wisdom. And in all your getting, get understanding"* (Proverbs 4:7). Years ago, when I began this journey, the Lord told me, *Larry, I am going to teach you how to reread the Bible through the eyes of a Jewish Jesus.* Jesus was not a Gentile Jesus, a Greek Jesus, a Roman Jesus, or an American Jesus; He was a Jewish Jesus. He thought Jewish, acted Jewish, and taught Jewish. He didn't come to do away with the law—the Torah— but to show us how it works and to make it come alive. He came to change God's Word from the *logos*, the written Word, to the *rhema*, the living Word! This is why God tells us to study— *"rightly dividing the word of truth"* (2 Timothy 2:15)—in order to discover for ourselves what Scripture says and what it means.

We Are Grafted In

In the book of Romans, the apostle Paul wrote to Gentile Christians, saying,

> *For I speak to you Gentiles; inasmuch as I am an apostle to the Gentiles....If some of the branches were broken off, and you, being a wild olive tree, were grafted in among them, and with them became a partaker of the root and fatness of the olive tree, do not boast against the branches. But if you do boast, remember that you do not support the root, but the root supports you. You will say then, "Branches were broken off that I might be grafted in."* (Romans 11:13, 17–19)

Very simply, we, the non-Jewish Christian church, are the wild branch. Israel, the land and its people, are the tree and the root into which we have been grafted. In later chapters, I'll discuss the prophecy concerning Israel becoming a nation again as a definite sign of the end times. For now, however, let's concentrate on the end of verse 17: *"a partaker of the root and fatness of the olive tree."*

In these last days, I believe that God is reconnecting the branch that is the church to its Jewish roots. As I write this, I think again of what that great rabbi said about the "children of miracles." At first, he said, other people would see this and think it strange. After all, many Christians have been taught that by sending Jesus, God did away with "all those Jewish things." Let me ask you, did God do away with *"You shall not commit adultery"* (Exodus 20:14)? Did He do away with *"You shall not steal"* (verse 15) or *"You shall have no other gods before Me"* (verse 3)? Aren't those all "Jewish things"?

When I first began to teach on our Jewish roots, most people thought that such teachings were irrelevant to Christians. Now, more than fifteen years later, I am still teaching these things to Christians all over the world.

Before I go any further, let me tell you how my marvelous journey into the secrets of God's Word began for me, my family, and my ministry. It is a story I first told in *The Torah Blessing*, but it bears repeating in order for you to understand my path.

My Awakening

Fifteen years ago, I found myself on my very first trip to Israel. It was not a trip I had been dying to make. After all, as a Christian, I had been taught that God was essentially done with Israel and that the Jews had received their chance to accept Jesus as Messiah but had blown it. I was taught that the "church"—not a denomination or building, but the believers who formed the body of Christ—had replaced Israel; in fact, the church *was* Israel.

I was so misguided. *Nothing* could have been further from the truth.

I certainly wasn't looking to "reconnect with my Jewish roots" on this trip. I wouldn't even have known what that phrase meant. I was, however, dealing with a gnawing feeling that, as a pastor, I dared not utter in the light of day: there was something missing in my life and in my Christian faith.

Have you ever felt like that? In your quiet, solitary moments, have you ever wondered or even prayed,

God, what's wrong?

I love You; I'm serving You; I believe Your Word.

I know that You are the same yesterday, today, and forever. I know it's all true.

So, why does it feel like something is missing in my life?

If you've ever struggled with those thoughts, you're not alone. I know exactly what you're going through. It was with this mind-set that I embarked on my trip to Israel.

After I arrived in the Holy Land, one of the first places my Israeli friends took me was Capernaum. Despite my hesitancy, I was truly excited to go there because I knew this to be the location of one of the great stories of the Bible. Capernaum was the place where Jesus healed Peter's mother-in-law, described in Mark 1:29–39.

As we walked through the gates, the remains of Peter's house were directly ahead of us. It's one of the most popular tourist attractions in all of Israel. Many people who go there, however, miss another spot of equal importance. Turn to your right after passing through the gates, and you will see the remains of an ancient synagogue. Joseph, my friend from Jerusalem, began to tell me all about this holy place of Jewish worship. As he did so, I couldn't help but think, *So what? What does this synagogue have to do with me? I'm a believer in Jesus.* Then, Joseph pointed out an inscription on the doorpost. It indicated that the synagogue had been dedicated by the grandchildren of the apostles of Jesus. As the group began to walk away, I remained transfixed. I stopped the group and said, "Joseph, tell me again who dedicated this synagogue."

He told me again.

"How can that be?" I asked. "Weren't the descendants of the apostles Christians? Weren't they followers of Jesus?"

Joseph said, "Of course, they were."

Still confused, I asked, "Then, what would a believer in Jesus be doing in a synagogue? Did they backslide?"

The next few words changed my life, and I believe they will change yours, too. It was the reason God had brought me to Israel. It was the answer I had been looking for.

> **Jesus never intended for His followers to be separated from Israel, from God's people, or from the Torah. As Christians, we were to be grafted in.**

"Larry," he said, "the church and the synagogue were synonymous for three hundred and twenty-five years after Christ's resurrection. Jesus never intended for His followers to be separated from Israel, from God's people, or from the Torah. As Christians, we were to be *grafted* in."

As Joseph led the rest of the group to Peter's house, I remained. I wasn't alone, though, for my God—the God of Israel, the God of the Jews, the God of that synagogue—was right there with me. He gently said to me, "Larry, I'm going to open your eyes. I'm going to teach you how to read My Word, not with the eyes of a Gentile Jesus, not with the eyes of a Protestant Jesus or a Catholic Jesus, but with the eyes of a Jewish Jesus. I'm going to show you what you've been missing."

Standing at the entrance of a two-thousand-year-old synagogue in Capernaum, Israel, on the Sea of Galilee, I was stunned by a profound revelation: Jesus was a Jew—a practicing, observant Jew. Not only that, but His disciples and followers were also practicing Jews.

For some, this may seem like a no-brainer, but for me, in that moment, I was struck with a revelation that completely altered my understanding of who Jesus was—and, therefore, who *I* was as a Christian. The inscription on that synagogue was a dedication by the Christian descendants of Jesus' disciples. For generations, the followers of Jesus had continued to attend synagogue, maintaining their observance of the Jewish faith and lifestyle.

That experience led me to see Jesus, and the entire Bible, in a fresh, new light. It was a paradigm shift—a total uprooting of how I had been taught to read the Word of God and how I had followed Jesus. As a result, it was a total shift in how I saw myself and lived my life as a Christian.

The journey I've since taken to uncover and understand the Jewish roots of my Christian faith has been, aside from the moment of my salvation, the most transformative, exciting, and fulfilling experience of my life. I began to read Scripture from a Jewish perspective rather than from the Greek- or Roman-influenced doctrine I had been taught as a young believer. I realized that Jesus and His disciples weren't *converted* Jews but rather *practicing* Jews—keepers of the Torah. I began to understand that, for a follower of Jesus, there is profound power and revelation in understanding the Torah—not only by studying it, but also by keeping and sharing in many of its customs and celebrations.

Your Awakening

Understand, I wasn't looking for a Jewish revelation, but God's Word promises that those *"who hunger and thirst for righteousness...shall be filled"* (Matthew 5:6). Once again, it is no accident that you're reading this book. God knows you are hungry and thirsty for more of Him. Perhaps, like me and so many others, you have been praying that God would fill you and quench your thirst, but you never dreamed that such a meal would come from a "kosher kitchen"! When you stop to think about it, why should it be such a surprise? The prophets, for the most part, were Jewish. The apostles were Jewish. Our Bible is Jewish. Oh, by the way, Jesus was Jewish, too!

The best way to read the Bible—a Jewish book—is to do so by thinking like a Jew. Let me help you in this. The starting point, the launching pad, to all that God has in store for you is a change in the way you see God and a change in the way you think God sees you. Again, I will show you how.

To close this chapter, I'd like you to hear from one of the pastors at our church, Scott Sigman, and his recollection of a prophecy from Bishop Donald Battle:

> I have the privilege of traveling with Pastor Huch as he preaches in other churches, as well as at conferences and on television programs. I am always amazed at the responses of people as Pastor teaches on reconnecting to our Jewish roots.
>
> Several years ago, while we were in Atlanta preaching for Bishop Donald Battle at his annual Pastors Conference, Pastor Larry taught an incredible sermon, "Healing in His Wings," that left the audience amazed because they had never heard such powerful revelation and Bible teaching before. Just as Pastor Larry ended and was ready to leave, Bishop Battle went to the microphone and began to prophesy about the future

of our ministry. He said, "Pastor Larry, what God is showing you, and what you're revealing, is a word and a message for the world for this hour! God is raising you up to be a daily voice to the world in order to teach His people this revelation of the Jewish roots to the Christian faith!"

Every day, I get more and more excited as the Lord unveils His Word and releases His miracles. Now, you are on this exciting journey with me!

The Return of Israel, Miracles, and the Messiah

In all my years of ministry, I have seldom taught on prophecy. There are a couple of reasons for this. First, when I hear people preach about prophecy, the message is often about doom and gloom and suffering in the end times. To be honest with you, I don't believe that we're going to go out suffering. I believe we're going to go out with a shout. My Bible says, *"When these things begin to happen, look up and lift up your heads, because your redemption draws near"* (Luke 21:28). Second, I know that you've never met anybody like this, but, sometimes, Christians can get a little "nutty." I've met people who believe that they are Ezekiel or Daniel or Michael, the archangel. When you venture into the area of prophecy, people can get sort of weird. The next thing you know, people are selling their homes, meeting in a field in the middle of the desert, and waiting for a spaceship! Jesus was very clear on this matter when He said, *"Of that day and hour no one knows, not even the angels of heaven, but My Father only"* (Matthew 24:36). No one knows when Jesus is coming back. In saying that, we may not know the exact moment, but God does give us signs so that we can be ready when it happens. The Bible refers to these signs as *"birth pains"* (Matthew 24:8 NIV).

When a woman visits her doctor and is confirmed to be pregnant, the doctor gives her a due date. Everybody knows that due dates are just an educated guess. No doctor can tell you the exact time. But when that time gets close, the mother gets signs, or birth pains, that tell you that you'd better pack your bags, know the way to the hospital, and make sure the car is filled with gas. These are signs to prepare women so that labor doesn't catch them unawares.

When our daughter, Anna, was born, that's how it worked. She was our first. When Tiz began to feel the birth pains, we went right to the hospital, and, in few hours, Anna was born. It didn't work that way for our son, Luke. It wasn't because God wasn't giving us the signs; it's because we weren't paying attention. We had just gone into full-time ministry and were starting a church in Santa Fe, New Mexico. Just before Luke's birth, however, I had been overseas for a few weeks. The day after I got home, Tiz said, "You know, I've been having some labor pains." I asked her, "Well, what do you think we should do?" She said, "Oh, they come and they go. It'll be all right." The next day was Sunday. We went to church in the morning and again that night. But after the evening service, the pains began again. I asked, "What do you think?" But Tiz said, "Oh, they'll go away," and they did. So, Monday morning, I asked again, "What do you think?" Once again, Tiz said, "Well, I'm feeling something, but it'll go away." Well, I had to be in court to testify on behalf of a young man who had been saved from gang activity. Tiz told me to go and insisted that she'd be fine. So, I went to the church to meet the assistant pastor and this young man I was going to support in court. As we were standing outside the church building, the assistant pastor's sister came running up the street, yelling, "Pastor! Pastor! Tiz just called. She's having the baby."

"Who's with her?" I asked.

She replied, "Nobody!"

I ran into the church and called the house to make sure this was correct. Anna was only three and a half years old, and she was told not to answer the phone because we often received phone calls from overseas. But after the phone rang once or twice, this little voice said, "Hello?"

I said, "Anna, where's your mom?!"

"Daddy, Daddy!" she said. "Guess what?"

"What?"

"Momma's having a baby."

"I know that, I know that! When?!"

"Right now!"

So, we jumped in the car. We were about fifteen minutes from the house, but we ran through stoplights and over side-walks to get there. I ran into the little trailer that was our home and saw Anna lying on the couch, crying. She hadn't expected to see a baby being born. I ran down the hallway, and, sure enough, here came Luke! The scene was pandemonium. We were freaking out. We were running all around, and the phone was ringing. It was the doctor.

He said, "I hear you're having a baby."

"Yeah," I said. "What do I do?"

"Call me when it's over."

Right there, with sirens blazing and Tiz screaming, we birthed Luke. I'm pretty sure I know what our neighbors were thinking: *I knew it. He killed her!*

By the time our third child, Katie, came, we were determined to pay attention to the signs. The moment Tiz said, "You know, I'm starting to feel—" I interrupted and said, "Get in the car! Get in the car!" I think we made ten or eleven trips to the hospital due to false alarms before Katie was finally born. We had learned with Luke, and we made it with Katie.

With Jesus' return, if we miss these signs, there will be another chance seven years later. But, trust me, you are going to want to respond the first time.

God has a powerful plan that He is unveiling to the world. It is a plan that will not only release signs, wonders, and miracles on His people but ultimately will also reveal the Messiah. One of the secrets to discovering how the power and the glory of the Lord will be ushered in is to go back and study the origins of our faith. Many of the ancient secrets of the Bible have been lost or hidden from us in our modern-day Christianity.

> **When we understand these earliest truths from the original teachings, we will release the power and promises of God into our lives.**

In some cases, we have been taught a different gospel, one meant to replace the foundational truths that were passed down since the days of Abraham, Isaac, and Jacob. Today, many believers in Jesus have yet to realize the importance of studying their faith from a Hebrew perspective. Little do they know that most of the sermons, doctrines, and teachings they receive have originated in Europe, not in Israel—the Holy Land.

When we understand these earliest truths from the original teachings, we will release the power and promises of God into our lives, the same kind of power we read about in the book of Acts. Ultimately, as we learn, study, develop, and grow in our knowledge of this revelation, it will prepare us—Christ's body, the church—for the return of our Messiah.

Replacement Theology

One of the key prophetic teachings we need to understand has to do with Israel. Many teachers and leaders within Christianity subscribe to the idea that the church has replaced Israel in God's plan, and that, therefore, Israel is no longer significant in Christian life.

Recently, one denomination with a worldwide member-ship formally declared that all the promises God gave to Israel were nullified with the coming of Jesus. This concept is com-monly referred to as "replacement theology." It has been taught in Christian churches for centuries throughout the Western world. But, as you will see as you read this book, Israel still plays a vital role in God's plan. The word God gave Abraham in Genesis 12:3 is still true today: *"I will bless those who bless you, and I will curse him who curses you."*

This prophecy, when understood from a Hebrew mind-set, will unlock untold blessings and revelations that can change your life and your church, as well as all of the nations of the world.

There is a Scripture that most pastors preach on at least once a year, if not more. We all know that when the pastor says, "Open your Bibles to Malachi...," we are in for a sermon on tithing.

> *"Return to Me, and I will return to you," says the LORD of hosts. "But you said, 'In what way shall we return?' Will a man rob God? Yet you have robbed Me! But you say, 'In what way have we robbed You?' In tithes and offerings."* (Malachi 3:7–8)

Here, God is talking about our faithfulness in giving our tithes and offerings. For now, let's not concentrate on the tith-ing part but on a powerful Jewish revelation found in one word: *return*. In Judaism, the Hebrew word for "returning" is *teshuvah*. God is calling out to the world—not only to the Jewish world, but to the entire world—saying, *"Return to Me, and I will return to you."*

When studying God's Word, the Jewish rabbis tell us that God's teachings always have two parts: the physical and the spiritual. Or, to put it another way, the teachings of God often have both an earthly meaning and a heavenly one.

Here's an example. Exodus 20:12 says, *"Honor your father and your mother, that your days may be long upon the land which the* LORD *your God is giving you."* Look at the companion Scripture from Ephesians 6:2: *"'Honor your father and mother,' which is the first commandment with promise: 'that it may be well with you and you may live long on the earth.'"* According to God, when we honor our fathers and mothers, He gives us not only a long life but also a good life—*"that it may be well with you."* Here, we have the first commandment that comes with a promise. Obeying it releases God's promise of a good, long life. At first glance, this may seem to be a verse about loving our physical fathers and mothers, those who birthed us into this world, fed us, and protected us. This, of course, is the physical, earthly side of this verse. But what about your spiritual parents? Look at what Paul wrote in 1 Corinthians 4:15:

> *For though you might have ten thousand instructors in Christ, yet you do not have many fathers; for in Christ Jesus I have begotten you through the gospel.*

Paul was saying that we have both physical and spiritual parents. So, in order to return to God—*teshuvah*—we must do so in two ways: physically and spiritually.

My good friend Rabbi Daniel Lapin says, "The first sign that a nation is cursed is that its children don't know who their fathers are." I think we would all agree that we are seeing this tragedy all over the world. There are multitudes of children worldwide who have no idea who their fathers are or have no relationships with them. Our society is filled with fatherless children. We see this in the physical, or natural, realm, but the same truth applies in the spiritual realm.

This is the deeper meaning of Malachi 4:5–6:

> *Behold I will send you Elijah the prophet before the coming of the great and dreadful day of the* LORD. *And he will turn the hearts of the fathers to the children, and the hearts of the children to their fathers, lest I come and strike the earth with a curse.*

Once again, this refers to both the physical hearts of fathers and their children, and to our spiritual fathers and children. We, as a Christian nation, need to understand who our fathers are. We know who our Messiah is, but do we know who our spiritual fathers are? The father of our faith is Abraham. Understanding this is the number one key to entering into the blessings of God. Abraham is our father, and we are heirs to the blessings of Abraham.

Isaiah 51 says,

Listen to Me, you who follow after righteousness, you who seek the LORD: look to the rock from which you were hewn, and to the hole of the pit from which you were dug. Look to Abraham your father, and to Sarah who bore you; for I called him alone, and blessed him and increased him. (verses 1–2)

That same word from God applies to us today! We still need to *"look to Abraham,"* our father, and to the covenant he made with God for all time, connecting him and his offspring to the Lord's blessings and increase! Remember, we are connecting the branches to the roots, the new to the old.

You might be thinking, *What does my faith today have to do with Abraham, who lived thousands of years ago?* We have to understand that when God makes a covenant, it doesn't fade away with time. The covenant that He made with Abraham was for all time!

For when God made a promise to Abraham, because He could swear by no one greater, He swore by Himself, saying, "Surely blessing I will bless you, and multiplying I will multiply you." (Hebrews 6:13–14)

For as many of you as were baptized into Christ have put on Christ. There is neither Jew nor Greek, there is neither slave nor free, there is neither male nor female; for you are all one in Christ Jesus. And if you are Christ's, then you are Abraham's seed, and heirs according to the promise. (Galatians 3:27–29)

> **You and I are Abraham's seed, his descendants, and heirs to his covenant promises from God.**

You and I are Abraham's seed, his descendants, and heirs to his covenant promises from God.

Now, let's look at the physical return to God. This could be the greatest miracle in all of biblical prophecy. God is fulfilling His promises to the nation of Israel, and that includes the return of God's people to the Promised Land from exile, where they had been scattered throughout the nations of the world.

Look at these prophecies in the Word of God:

Now it shall come to pass in the latter days that the mountain of the Lord's house shall be established on the top of the mountains, and shall be exalted above the hills; and all nations shall flow to it. Many people shall come and say, "Come, and let us go up to the mountain of the LORD, to the house of the God of Jacob; He will teach us His ways, and we shall walk in His paths." For out of Zion shall go forth the law, and the word of the LORD from Jerusalem. (Isaiah 2:2–3)

Now it shall come to pass in the latter days that the mountain of the Lord's house shall be established on the top of the mountains, and shall be exalted above the hills; and peoples shall flow to it. Many nations shall come and say, "Come, and let us go up to the mountain of the LORD, to the house of the God of Jacob; He will teach us His ways, and we shall walk in His paths." For out of Zion the law shall go forth, and the word of the LORD from Jerusalem. (Micah 4:1–2)

Another Hebrew word that refers to the return of the Jews to the land of Israel is the word *aliyah*. Specifically, *aliyah* is to ascend or rise. In the synagogue, it is used to describe the one who is given the great honor of reading the Torah. This person is called to *aliyah*—to ascend—to the platform to read the scrolls. If you're reading this book, it is God's call to you to ascend, or arise, spiritually, and receive the revelation and understanding of the Jewish roots of your faith. As in everything, *aliyah* has both a spiritual and a physical meaning.

Physically, it also refers to the return of Israel from exile in Egypt, and again from exile in Babylon; the return—*aliyah*—we have seen in the last century has never been seen before. Let's look at recent history and see what it has shown us.

The first *aliyah* in modern times began in the late 1800s and lasted almost thirty years. Jews from Russia and other areas in Eastern Europe fled the pogroms and persecutions in two great waves, with an estimated thirty-five thousand returning to Israel by 1904 and another forty thousand by 1914. Then, in 1923, another forty thousand Jews returned as the nation of Israel began its rise from the ruins.

By the end of the 1920s, an estimated eighty-two thousand escaped economic crisis and persecution in Poland and Hungary. Finally, because of the rise of Hitler and Nazism in Germany in the 1930s and 1940s, more than two hundred fifty thousand European Jews fled persecution and returned to Israel. Even though their land was under British control throughout that time, the atmosphere was dangerous for the Jewish people, and strict immigration guidelines were imposed. By the time Israel was declared a state by the United Nations in 1948, more than six hundred fifty thousand Jews had immigrated back to Israel.

The Proclamation of the Establishment of the State of Israel included the following:

> The state of Israel will be open for Jewish immigration and for the Ingathering of the Exiles; it will foster the development of the country for the benefit of all its

inhabitants; it will be based on freedom, justice and peace as envisaged by the prophets of Israel; it will ensure complete equality of social and political rights to all its inhabitants irrespective of religion, race or sex; it will guarantee freedom of religion, conscience, language, education and culture; it will safeguard the Holy Places of all religions; and it will be faithful to the principles of the Charter of the United Nations.[1]

This was followed in 1950 by the Law of Return, which granted every Jew the automatic right to immigrate to Israel and become a citizen of this new state. Following this law, the Jewish population more than doubled as immigrants, including survivors of the Holocaust, came from all the nations of the world.

By any historical measure, the nation of Israel should have disappeared long ago. The very survival of the Jewish people throughout recorded time is nothing short of miraculous. The fact that Israel today exists as a nation stands as testimony to the existence of a God who acts in history.

Winston Churchill said, "Some people like the Jews, and some do not. But no thoughtful man can deny the fact that they are, beyond any question, the most formidable and the most remarkable race which has appeared in the world."[2]

Mark Twain, the great American writer, who was an agnostic and a self-acknowledged skeptic, wrote,

> The Egyptian, the Babylonian, and the Persian rose, filled the planet with sound and splendour, then faded to dream-stuff and passed away; the Greek and the Roman followed, and made a vast noise, and they are gone; other peoples have sprung up and held their torch high for a time, but it burned out, and they sit in twilight now, or have vanished. The Jew saw

---

[1]The Declaration of the Establishment of the State of Israel, May 14, 1948: http://www.mfa.gov. il/MFA/Peace%20Process/Guide%20to%20the%20Peace%20Process/Declaration%20of%20 Establishment%20of%20State%20of%20Israel.
[2]Quoted by Geoffrey Wheatcroft in *The Controversy of Zion* (London: Sinclair-Stevenson, 1996), xi.

them all, beat them all, and is now what he always was, exhibiting no decadence, no infirmities of age, no weakening of his parts, no slowing of his energies, no dulling of his alert and aggressive mind. All things are mortal to the Jew; all other forces pass, but he remains. What is the secret of his immortality?[3]

The secret is found in the prophetic words spoken over the nation of Israel. If God decrees a thing, no nation, emperor, enemy, or religious doctrine can prevent it from coming to pass.

For thousands of years, Jewish people all over the world have held a Passover dinner, which is called the *seder*. This is the time to celebrate the miracle of God bringing Israel out of Egypt. At the end of each *seder*, the participants always say, "Next year in Jerusalem!" For thousands of years, that was the prayer. When we celebrate Passover, not only do we remember how the grace of God brought Israel out of centuries of bondage, but we also look forward to when God will bring us all together in the city of cities, Jerusalem.

> **If God decrees a thing, no nation, emperor, enemy, or religious doctrine can prevent it from coming to pass.**

The prophet Jeremiah spoke about the day when God would change the way in which Jews would speak of the miracle of the Exodus:

> *"Therefore behold, the days are coming," says the* LORD, *"that it shall no more be said, 'The* LORD *lives who brought up the children of Israel from the land of Egypt,' but, 'The* LORD *lives who brought up the children of Israel from the land of the north and from all the lands where He had driven them.' For I will bring them back into their land which I gave to their fathers."*
>
> (Jeremiah 16:14–15)

---

[3]Mark Twain, "Concerning the Jews," *Harper's Monthly Magazine*, September 1899. See also Charles Neider, ed., *The Complete Essays of Mark Twain* (New York: Doubleday & Company, 1963), 249.

This prophecy, even though it was about three thousand years old, came to pass on May 14, 1948. God said, in effect, "There will come a time when the people of Israel will not remember only that I delivered them out of Egypt but also that I delivered them from the nations of the world—from Russia, from Poland, from Germany, from wherever they were. They will say, 'Remember when God delivered us by a miracle? We are no longer exiles. God gave us back our land!'"

The miracle of leaving Egypt three thousand years ago pales in comparison to what we have seen God do in this past century by bringing Jews back to Israel from all over the world. There has never been a time in the history of the world when a people have been cast out of their country and into the whole world for two thousand years, only to return again. God gave us a prophecy that His people, who wouldn't even know each other and had no connection with each other, would all return to their homeland and rebuild their country.

Look with me at the prophecy in Ezekiel 37:

The hand of the LORD came upon me and brought me out in the Spirit of the LORD, and set me down in the midst of the valley; and it was full of bones. Then He caused me to pass by them all around, and behold, there were very many in the open valley; and indeed they were very dry. And He said to me, "Son of man, can these bones live?" So I answered, "O Lord GOD, You know." Again He said to me, "Prophesy to these bones, and say to them, 'O dry bones, hear the word of the LORD! Thus says the Lord GOD to these bones: "Surely I will cause breath to enter into you, and you shall live. I will put sinews on you and bring flesh upon you, cover you with skin and put breath in you; and you shall live. Then you shall know that I am the LORD."'"…
Then He said to me, "Son of man, these bones are the whole house of Israel. They indeed say, 'Our bones are dry, our hope is lost, and we ourselves are cut off!'

Therefore prophesy and say to them, 'Thus says the Lord GOD: "Behold, O My people, I will open your graves and cause you to come up from your graves, and bring you into the land of Israel."'" (Ezekiel 37:1–6, 11–12)

Christians often use this passage to illustrate how God can resurrect our dreams and destinies through His Word. And that's valid. If someone is facing obstacles in a marriage, finances, or health, he can speak the Word of the Lord to his circumstances and apply this principle from Ezekiel to his life. But the prophet is also talking about the land and the people of Israel. He says, in effect, "Israel, you look dead. Can you live?" God was saying to Ezekiel, "These bones have no flesh, no heart, and no lungs. My land has no people, no government, no leaders, and no army. But I say to you that these bones shall live." Ezekiel replied, "God, only You would know." In other words, this is such a miracle, God alone could perform it.

This is why the prophet Isaiah said, *"Who has heard such a thing? Who has seen such things? Shall the earth be made to give birth in one day? Or shall a nation be born at once? For as soon as Zion was in labor, she gave birth to her children"* (Isaiah 66:8).

"Therefore, behold, the days are coming," says the LORD, "that they shall no longer say, 'As the LORD lives who brought up the children of Israel from the land of Egypt,' but, 'As the LORD lives who brought up and led the descendants of the house of Israel from the north country and from all the countries where I had driven them.' And they shall dwell in their own land."

(Jeremiah 23:7–8)

If God said Israel will become a nation, Israel will become a nation. If God said, "I'll bring them back to their Promised Land from all around the world," then it will happen. If God said, "By My stripes, you are healed," then you're healed. (See Isaiah 53:5.) What seems impossible, God will make happen.

What's impossible for man is not impossible for God. Could Israel actually return? Could God actually restore Israel to the Promised Land almost two thousand years later? In 1948, the miracle became official as Israel was acknowledged as a nation.

In Genesis 12:3, God promised Abram that He would bless those who blessed him and curse those who cursed him. I believe that, for two thousand years, the church has been under a curse because we've been taught that our institution has replaced Israel. We've been under a curse because we have blamed Israel. We've been under a curse because we've persecuted Israel. But God is about to reverse the curse. Just as the world witnessed the miracle of God bringing the Jews back to Israel, it is now witnessing the miracle of God bringing the church back to Israel.

> **Just as the world witnessed the miracle of God bringing the Jews back to Israel, it is now witnessing the miracle of God bringing the church back to Israel.**

All around the world, Christians are beginning to embrace and love Israel. They are beginning to love the Jewish people of Israel. This is not just a new experience for the Christian church; it's also a new experience for the Jews. It's the end-time miracle of *teshuvah*—the return. God is using Christians like you and me, who have returned to our Jewish roots, to repair a relationship that has been damaged for centuries. We are tearing down the walls that divide.

Look at Isaiah 58:9–12:

> *Then you shall call, and the LORD will answer; you shall cry, and He will say, "Here I am." If you take away the yoke from your midst, the pointing of the finger, and speaking wickedness, if you extend your soul to the hungry and satisfy the afflicted soul, then your light shall dawn in the darkness, and your darkness shall be as the noonday. The LORD will guide you continually,*

and satisfy your soul in drought, and strengthen your bones; you shall be like a watered garden, and like a spring of water, whose waters do not fail. Those from among you shall build the old waste places; you shall raise up the foundations of many generations; and you shall be called the Repairer of the Breach, the Restorer of Streets to Dwell In.

God is ready to return. Everywhere we look, we see the signs. The Messiah is ready to set up His kingdom in Jerusalem, where He will rule and reign forever. But first, there will be a return to Israel—not just a physical return of people to their land but also a spiritual return, an *aliyah*, when believers will ascend spiritually to the Jewish origins of God's Word. Malachi 4:6 will be fulfilled as God "[turns] *the hearts of the fathers to the children, and the hearts of the children to their fathers.*" Around the world, this spiritual return is already beginning to take place. The end-time prophecy is that our hearts will turn back toward the fathers of our faith, Abraham, Isaac, and Jacob.

This is the fulfillment of what Paul wrote in Ephesians 2:12–15:

At that time you were without Christ, being aliens from the commonwealth of Israel and strangers from the covenants of promise, having no hope and without God in the world. But now in Christ Jesus you who once were far off have been brought near by the blood of Christ. For He Himself is our peace, who has made both one, and has broken down the middle wall of separation, having abolished in His flesh the enmity, that is, the law of commandments contained in ordinances, so as to create in Himself one new man from the two, thus making peace.

We are seeing the formation of that *"one new man."* Paul further explained this in his epistle to the Romans, where he described the proper way to view the relationship between Jew and Gentile:

And if some of the branches were broken off, and you,
being a wild olive tree, were grafted in among them,
and with them became a partaker of the root and fat-
ness of the olive tree, do not boast against the branches.
But if you do boast, remember that you do not support
the root, but the root supports you. (Romans 11:17–18)

God has not rejected the Jewish people. Rather, they are
the root that supports everything else. When we understand,
we ascend, not just physically but also spiritually, to God's
Word, so that the mysteries may be unveiled and the miracles
may be released.

When I was invited to speak at one of the Jewish synagogues here in Dallas, I did not know what kind of response to
expect from the congregation. I had forged a friendship with the
rabbis over the previous several years that had begun with a
service that we had called "Night to Honor Israel." But earning
the trust of the Jewish community is not an easy thing. It is not
difficult to understand why there is a lot of mistrust and skep-
ticism in the minds of most Jewish people toward Christians.
They have been the targets of so much persecution over many
centuries, a fact that still affects their view of Christianity.

Several years ago, Tiz and I took a tour group to Israel.
During our visit, we saw a beautiful ring in the window of the
King David Hotel. It had Hebrew writing on it that said, "As
you open your hand to help people, you draw God near to you.
As you close your hand to help people, you push God away
from you." Tiz and I were really moved by this saying on this
ring. So, as a surprise for my fiftieth birthday, Tiz contacted the
Israeli artist and had one made for me. Tiz told the artist that
we were Christian pastors who teach people about the Jewish
roots of Christianity, and that we have a love for the nation and
the people of Israel. The artist, Janet, was astounded and said,
"I don't understand this. Don't you, as Christians, hate us, as
Jews? Everything I know about Christians, from history and

from the news, makes me think that Christians are our ene-
mies and that they are out to destroy us. I have always thought
that Christians wanted to steal our souls and destroy us as a
people. What makes you and your husband want to embrace us
and reach out to us?"

Tiz shared with her that our mission is to tear down the
walls that divide and to bring the Christian world back to its
Jewish roots. A wonderful friendship and connection came
about and has developed over the past few years.

Golda's Story

On the night I spoke at the synagogue, I gained a vivid
insight into how big the job of tearing down the walls that have
divided us for generations will be. But, I also saw how easy it
is for you and me to begin tearing them down. The rabbis had
asked me to speak on that very subject: "Tearing Down the
Walls That Divide and Building a Bridge." The goal of my talk
was for all of us to focus on what we have in common. In one
hour, I tried to teach on the very things I am laying out in this
book. By the end, the rabbis asked if we could open up the
service for questions and discussion from the congregation. In
fact, one rabbi smiled and told the attendees, "Ask any and
all the questions you want!" To my great joy, these wonderful people bombarded me with sincere questions, wanting to
know all about why I was teaching on the Jewish roots of the
Christian faith. It was an incredible evening, and we could all
feel the walls of division crumbling down.

Afterward, Tiz spoke to a lovely woman named Golda who
was deeply moved by the event. With tears in her eyes, she told
her story to Tiz:

> I was born and raised in a Jewish home in Montreal,
> Canada. I am approaching seventy years old. I love
> God with all my heart, keep all the Jewish holidays,
> and come to Synagogue two or three times a week. I

have raised all my children the same way. We have a wonderful, loving family. But, in all my years and in all my travels, I have never heard anything like what I heard tonight! My whole life I have deliberately kept away from Christian people because I truly thought they hated me as a Jew.

My first experience with "Christians" was as a little child in my neighborhood in Montreal. My family was the only Jewish family in the neighborhood. I remember as if it was yesterday when the neighborhood children would surround me and shout, "You little dirty Jew! Go home, you swine Jew girl!" They would taunt and chase me endlessly until I was horrified to leave my house. From that time on, nearly seventy years, my view of Christians has been colored by those experiences. I assumed that all of them felt this way about us, as Jews.

Consequently, I taught my children and my grandchildren to think and react the same way in their lives. We have kept our distance and separation from the Christian world and never had any desire or reason to do otherwise.

For three generations, we have lived with these walls of division. But now, for the first time ever, I am hearing that you love me and care about me! I can't even tell you how deeply this is impacting me. This night has changed my life and my children's and grandchildren's lives forever! Thank you and your people, Pastor Huch, for coming here to speak with us and for showing us your love and God's love! God bless you!

As Golda and Tiz wept together, Tiz reached out and embraced her, saying, "Let me be the first Christian to give you a hug!" With a simple message and act of love, hundreds of years of walls that had divided came tumbling down for the generations to come. And let me say that these walls were not built by God but by the misconceptions and cruelties of mankind. It is time for all of God's people to tear down the walls that divide and work together to usher in the great outpouring of the last days!

PART
II

Unveiling the Pathway
to Prosperity

Pathway to Prosperity:
From the Desert to the Promised Land

Therefore you shall keep the commandments of the Lord your God, to walk in His ways and to fear Him. For the Lord your God is bringing you into a good land, a land of brooks of water, of fountains and springs, that flow out of valleys and hills; a land of wheat and barley, of vines and fig trees and pomegranates, a land of olive oil and honey; a land in which you will eat bread without scarcity, in which you will lack nothing; a land whose stones are iron and out of whose hills you can dig copper. When you have eaten and are full, then you shall bless the Lord your God for the good land which He has given you. Beware that you do not forget the Lord your God by not keeping His commandments, His judgments, and His statutes which I command you today, lest; when you have eaten and are full, and have built beautiful houses and dwell in them; and when your herds and your flocks multiply, and your silver and your gold are multiplied, and all that you have is multiplied; when your heart is lifted up, and you forget the Lord your God who brought you out of the land of Egypt, from the house of bondage; who led you through that great and terrible wilderness, in which were fiery serpents and scorpions and thirsty land where there was no water; who brought water for you out of the flinty rock; who fed you in the wilderness with manna, which your fathers did not know, that He might humble you and that He might test you, to do you good in the end; then you say in your heart, "My power and the might of my hand have gained me this wealth." And you shall remember the Lord your God, for it is He who gives you power to get wealth, that He may establish His covenant which He swore to your fathers, as it is this day.

(Deuteronomy 8:6–18)

In this section, I will equip you to break the curse of poverty and release the blessing of prosperity. I will show you that it is not God's plan and will for you to live in scarcity, lack, and insufficiency. Rather, it is His will that you live in abundance, overflow, and prosperity. Are you ready to come out of the desert and enter into the Promised Land—the land that was promised to our forefathers? Come with me as I lay out the pathway to prosperity. May I be your guide into the Promised Land?

Between Captivity and the Promised Land

Deuteronomy 8 describes a major turning point in Jewish history. God's people had been wandering in the desert for forty years because of fear and unbelief. The desert was better than slavery in Egypt, but it was not God's best. Finally, the Lord declared that the Israelites were ready to leave the desert and enter into the Promised Land. God had taken care of them in the desert, feeding them manna and leading them to water, but those years had been a time of barely getting by. God had declared that the Promised Land would be *"a good land, a land of brooks of water, of fountains and springs, that flow out of valleys and hills; a land of wheat and barley, of vines and fig trees and pomegranates, a land of olive oil and honey; a land…without scarcity."* This was a land in which they would lack nothing.

Because of their unbelief and disobedience, however, God's people had been missing out on all that He had intended them to have all along. They were paying the consequences for not keeping the commandments of God.

Finally, the day came when they would be able to leave the desert, once and for all. It was time to go in and possess the land that God had promised them. It was time for them to connect to His covenant of blessings!

Likewise, now is *your* time to come out of your desert, and out of a life of "barely enough," once and for all! It is *your* time to connect to God's covenant of blessings for *your* life! Now, let me show you a powerful secret that explains why.

Before God's people entered the Promised Land, Moses told his father-in-law, *"We are setting out for the place of which the LORD said, 'I will give it to you.'…Please do not leave, inasmuch as you know how we are to camp in the wilderness, and you can be our eyes"* (Numbers 10:29, 31). But his father-in-law, a Gentile, declined, saying, *"I will not go, but I will depart to my own land and to my relatives"* (verse 30). In other words, he declined to enter into the Promised Land without going back to get his own people.

> **Now is *your* time to come out of your desert, and out of a life of "barely enough," once and for all! It is *your* time to connect to God's covenant of blessings for *your* life!**

One of the questions I'm asked whenever I teach among Jewish people is, "You understand the Jewishness of the Bible more than many of us do. Why don't you just come with us?" My response is the same as Moses' father-in-law's: "I'm coming with you, but, first, I must go back and get my own people. I have to go back and get the Christians." God intends for Jews and Gentiles to go into the Promised Land together. I believe that we, as Christians, are about to go into a Promised Land of prosperity, a land flowing with milk and honey. Most Jews don't believe in a doctrine of poverty. They believe in the covenant of prosperity. In this section, I'm going to take you through the last part of the desert and into the Promised Land with the

Jewish people so that, together, we can enjoy the land that flows with milk and honey!

When God spoke to Moses through the burning bush, He explained that His people would remain in captivity for a certain time, but that when that time ended, He would take them on a journey to the Promised Land. And they would not be going on that journey empty-handed but with all of the silver and gold of Egypt.

> *I will stretch out My hand and strike Egypt with all My wonders which I will do in its midst; and after that he will let you go. And I will give this people favor in the sight of the Egyptians; and it shall be, when you go, that you shall not go empty-handed. But every woman shall ask of her neighbor, namely, of her who dwells near her house, articles of silver, articles of gold, and clothing; and you shall put them on your sons and on your daughters. So you shall plunder the Egyptians.*
>
> (Exodus 3:20–22)

Ancient Jewish teachings say that when Moses was getting ready to lead the people out of Egypt, God told him, "Beg My people. Do not leave without the silver and the gold." Now, stop and think about this. Why would God even have to tell Moses to be sure the people left with all the wealth of the Egyptians? Why did God ask Moses to beg His people not to leave without the silver and the gold? It is because the people were so excited about their freedom—about no longer being enslaved—that that would have been enough for them. It was enough just to be free. But God insisted that the transfer of wealth from the bank accounts of the wicked into the hands of the children of God was to be part of their redemption.

How many of us think that it's enough to receive forgiveness and know we're on our way to heaven? But God is saying, in effect, "No! I want you to experience the last part of this journey. I want you to take the silver and the gold because this is the second part of your redemption." This is the great transfer of wealth into your hands. It is God adding to your freedom the blessing of prosperity. Deuteronomy 8 says, *"And you shall remember the LORD your God, for it is He who gives you power to get wealth, that He may establish His covenant"* (verse 18). We need to realize that we have a covenant of prosperity with God.

In the New Testament, God has given us a blood covenant through Jesus Christ to receive all of His promises—including prosperity.

> *In Him we have redemption through His blood, the forgiveness of sins, according to the riches of His grace.*
> (Ephesians 1:7)

Now, let me show you another secret concerning what it means to be redeemed.

We have been redeemed by the blood of the Lamb. When I preach, I often say, "Finish this phrase: 'We are redeemed by the _____.'" In response, people usually shout, "Blood!" Then, I ask, "Where did Jesus shed His blood?" To this, most people answer, "At Calvary." Then, I show them the revelation that Jesus didn't shed His blood just once but seven different times.

> *He shall take some of the blood of the bull and sprinkle it with his finger on the mercy seat on the east side; and before the mercy seat he shall sprinkle some of the blood with his finger seven times.* (Leviticus 16:14)

To be *redeemed* is to be "bought back" or to be "seen again." In other words, it is to be taken back to the garden of Eden, where we are seen again as children of the covenant. That's why one of the seven "places" where Jesus shed His blood was when He was made to wear the crown of thorns. This was to break the curse of poverty. Let me illustrate for you the curse of poverty and the resulting separation from God.

Also for Adam and his wife the LORD God made tunics of skin, and clothed them. Then the LORD God said, "Behold, the man has become like one of Us, to know good and evil. And now, lest he put out his hand and take also of the tree of life, and eat, and live forever...."   (Genesis 3:21–22)

Then, God drove them out, removing them from the garden.

...Therefore the LORD God sent him out of the garden of Eden to till the ground from which he was taken. So He drove out the man; and He placed cherubim at the east of the garden of Eden, and a flaming sword which turned every way, to guard the way to the tree of life.   (verses 23–24)

In these two verses, it says the same thing twice: God sent Adam and Eve out, and then He drove them out. In Hebrew, whenever you find two of something or read of something being taught twice, it's because there is a secret revelation that God is trying to unveil.

Here, God is revealing something physical and something spiritual. First, in verse 23, God physically removed man from the garden, a land of abundance that flowed with milk and honey. Then, in verse 24, He drove man out from the garden. This was a spiritual removal. Ancient Jewish wisdom says that God divorced Himself from Adam and Eve, and from mankind, so that, for them, He ceased to be *Jehovah Jireh*, their Provider. In the garden, even though man worked by sowing seed and tilling the ground, it was his covenant relationship with God that caused everything he did to prosper. When God removed Adam and Eve from the garden, they were removed from His presence physically, and they were also removed from His provision spiritually. They were cast out of the garden and into a curse of poverty.

Cursed is the ground for your sake; in toil you shall eat of it all the days of your life. Both thorns and thistles it shall bring forth for you, and you shall eat the herb of the field. (Genesis 3:17–18)

God cursed the land with thorns and thistles. The sweat on Adam's brow symbolized that no matter how much seed was sown, no matter how much land was tilled, and no matter how many tasks were completed, God was no longer *Jehovah Jireh*; the covenant of abundance was no longer in effect. Thus, the thorn became a symbol of the curse of poverty. This is why the soldiers took branches from a thorn bush and wove them into a crown, piercing Jesus with it as they placed it on His head. Jesus was crowned with the symbol of the curse of poverty. When the crown drew blood on the brow of Jesus, we became reconnected to the covenant of prosperity and abundance. This is why it says in Deuteronomy 8:18, *"It is [God] who gives you power to get wealth, that He may establish His covenant."* Redemption is not just being saved and delivered; it's also reconnecting to the covenant in which *"the wealth of the sinner is stored up for the righteous"* (Proverbs 13:22) and put into your hands.

Why was it that as the Jews left Egypt, the people there gave them all their silver and gold? It's because the Egyptians owed the Jews four hundred years' worth of back wages.

In this psalm, the psalmist wrote honestly from his heart to the Lord, expressing an attitude we may harbor from time to time:

Truly God is good to Israel, to such as are pure in heart. But as for me, my feet had almost stumbled; my steps had nearly slipped. For I was envious of the boastful, when I saw the prosperity of the wicked. For there are no pangs in their death, but their strength is firm. They are not in trouble as other men, nor are they plagued like other men. Therefore pride serves as their necklace; violence covers them like a garment. Their eyes bulge with abundance; they have more than heart could wish. They scoff and speak *wickedly concerning oppression; they speak loftily. They set their mouth against the heavens, and their tongue walks through the earth. Therefore his people return here, and waters of a full cup are drained by them. And they say, "How does God know? And is there knowledge in the Most High?" Behold, these are the ungodly, who are always at ease; they increase in riches. Surely I have cleansed my heart in vain, and washed my hands in innocence. For all day long I have been plagued, and chastened every morning. If I had said, "I will speak thus," behold, I would have been untrue to the generation of Your children. When I thought how to understand this, it was too painful for me; until I went into the sanctuary of God; then I understood their end.* (Psalm 73:1–17)*

Have you ever felt this way? He said, in effect, "Lord, I know You're a good God, but there is something that is causing me to stumble. I see the wicked with all the money and all the prosperity. They are prosperous, full of pride, and their eyes bulge with abundance. Their cups are full and running over. God, why do they have all this, while Your children have nothing? It's too painful to see." Then, in verse 17, he entered the sanctuary of God and understood how it all would end.

Now, let's look at the fulfillment of Psalm 73 in James 5:

Come now, you rich, weep and howl for your miseries that are coming upon you! Your riches are corrupted, and your garments are moth-eaten. Your gold and silver are corroded, and their corrosion will be a witness against you and will eat your flesh like fire. You have heaped up treasure in the last days. Indeed the wages of the laborers who mowed your fields, which you kept back by fraud, cry out; and the cries of the reapers have reached the ears of the Lord of Sabaoth.

You have lived on the earth in pleasure and luxury; you have fattened your hearts as in a day of slaughter. You have condemned, you have murdered the just; he does not resist you. Therefore be patient, brethren, until the coming of the Lord. See how the farmer waits for the precious fruit of the earth, waiting patiently for it until it receives the early and latter rain. (James 5:1–7)

This passage forecasts the end-time transfer of wealth. Look specifically at verse 4: *"Indeed the wages of the laborers who mowed your fields, which you kept back by fraud, cry out."* James was referring to those in the world who have stolen the blessings of the children of God. *"Come now, you rich, weep and howl for your miseries that are coming upon you!"* He did not say that there was anything wrong with being wealthy. He was writing about those who had gotten rich by defrauding others. *"Your gold and silver are corroded, and their corrosion will be a witness against you and will eat your flesh like fire. You have heaped up treasure in the last days."* This is a prophecy concerning you and me. Just

> **When we realize that it's not God's will for us to continually struggle under financial burdens or to be deeply in debt to the world, we will cry out.**

as the Israelites left Egypt with all of the gold and silver, the end-time transfer of wealth from the wicked into the hands of the righteous will be a testimony of God's favor before the whole world. *"You have heaped up treasure in the last days. Indeed the wages of the laborers who mowed your fields, which you kept back by fraud, cry out; and the cries of the reapers have reached the ears of the Lord of Sabaoth."* Most Christians do not read this verse correctly and say "Sabbath" instead of *"Sabaoth."* The word *sabaoth* refers to the captain of armies or of hosts, or, better yet, the master avenger. So, in the very last days, here are the children of God, crying out and saying, "God, it's not right that we're just getting by. We're Your children." When we realize that it's not God's will for us to continually struggle under financial burdens or to be deeply in debt to the world, we will cry out. When we finally realize that we are to be the head and not the tail, above only and not beneath, the lender rather than the borrower, God will do for us exactly what He did for the people of Israel as they left Egypt.

Identifying the Real Thief

Why did the Israelites deserve the silver and the gold from the Egyptians? Because the Egyptians owed them four hundred years' worth of back wages. What does the world owe you? The "master avenger" is going to return everything you've lost. The thief is not the person who ripped you off in a business deal. That individual was merely a tool whom the devil used. The thief is the devil himself. Jesus said, *"The thief does not come except to steal, and to kill, and to destroy. I have come that they may have life, and that they may have it more abundantly"* (John 10:10).

If you're an African-American and your ancestors were enslaved and made to work without compensation, that wealth has been stored up for you. If one of your family members invented something lucrative and didn't get credit for it, everything he or she should have earned is being stored up and released to you. If you're a woman and you have been passed over for promotion or paid less for doing the same work as a man, you need to claim what your female ancestors never had. If you're Mexican-American and all your family has ever known is poverty and minimum-wage jobs, you need to claim access to better opportunities. If you're Native American, you need to claim the wealth your grandparents should have had. If you're Asian-American and America built the railroads on the backs of your ancestors, God hears your cry.

When you discover who the real thief is, he will have to pay you back seven times what he has stolen. If somebody has ripped you off, stolen from you, or cheated you, remember that

*"we do not wrestle against flesh and blood, but against princi-
palities, against powers, against the rulers of the darkness of
this age, against spiritual hosts of wickedness in the heavenly
places"* (Ephesians 6:12). People are tools. If we are in the hands
of the Carpenter, we are building up people's lives. But if we're
in the hands of the devil, we will destroy people's lives.

Here is something I teach all the time. If I lay hands on
you and you are healed, who healed you? Of course, God did.
But if I lay hands on you and steal from you, who stole from
you? Most people would say that *I* was the one doing the stealing. Why is it that we are spiritual enough to give God the
glory when a miracle happens, but we haven't learned to give
the devil blame when calamity strikes? People are simply tools.
We're either tools in the hands of God or tools in the hands of
the devil. This is why the Bible says, *"We do not wrestle against
flesh and blood, but against principalities, against powers,
against the rulers of the darkness of this age."*

The thief is not that man or woman who stabbed you in
the back, that business partner who defrauded you, or that
organization that mistreated you. The thief is the devil. Once
you understand that it's the devil who has been stealing your
blessing, he will have to pay back everything he has stolen from
you, multiplied by seven.

Here's a faith-building exercise: sit down with a pen and
paper and figure out how much has been stolen from you over
the years. How much has been stolen from you by unscrupu-
lous family members, teachers, bosses, or "friends"? Realize
that Satan was actually the one who stole these things and then
claim them back. Tell Satan you want everything that's been
stolen over all the years—with interest, multiplied by seven.

Your God-Given Desire

Now, through the blood of Jesus and the covenants
of prosperity and success, *"the LORD your God will bless*

you in all your works and in all to which you put your hand" (Deuteronomy 15:10).

We know that Scripture says to *"delight yourself also in the* Lord, *and He shall give you the desires of your heart"* (Psalm 37:4). But I want to show you what this really means in Hebrew terms of thinking. When you begin to desire something— assuming, of course, that it is according to God's will—the reason you want it is that He put that desire in your heart. The desire to build a business or to prosper and make more money or to have a nicer car or home is not evil. This is God's nature. The God we serve is not the God of "getting by"; He is the God of abundance. So, when you begin to desire these things, it's because God has put these desires in your heart.

Why is this important? Because the Bible says, *"He who doubts is like a wave of the sea driven and tossed by the wind. For let not that man suppose that he will receive anything from the Lord; he is a double-minded man, unstable in all his ways"* (James 1:6–8). The enemy will never tell you that God *can't* bring wealth into your life. We see it all around us. I certainly see it in Dallas, and it's wonderful: glass skyscrapers, a billion-dollar football stadium, luxury cars, and beautiful homes. We all know that wealth is out there, and yet, many Christians don't think that it is for them. We know God can provide wealth, but we don't think He'll do it for us. In fact, many Christians have been taught that even wishing for wealth is evil. We're double-minded. And when we're double-minded, we don't receive anything.

Perhaps you desire to build a business. You would like to have people working for you instead of always having to work for someone else. You desire to be the lender and not the bor- rower. God has put these desires in your heart. Unfortunately, you may have been told that being a Christian and being a businessperson do not go hand in hand. You need to realize that when Deuteronomy says, *"God will bless you in all your works and in all to which you put your hand,"* it means that God gave you the anointing to make money.

Twice in the book of Revelation, it says that we are anointed to be *"kings and priests"* (Revelation 1:6; 5:10). It's time for the church to embrace this truth. When I teach on Sunday mornings, I rely on the anointing of God in order to do what He has called me to do. The same is true for those of you who aren't in the ministry. I'm anointed by God to be a priest. You're anointed by God to be a king or queen. You're anointed by God to make money. This is why the Lord told Moses to beg his people to be sure to leave with all of Egypt's silver and gold, so that Israel would not become "double-minded."

Jesus even talked about this in His parable of the talents from Luke 19. In the parable, a nobleman gave each of his servants ten minas, or talents, and went away. While he was gone, two of the servants used the talents to make even more. This pleased the nobleman, who rewarded them with even more wealth and responsibility. To the wealthiest, he said, *"Well done, good servant; because you were faithful in a very little, have authority over ten cities"* (Luke 19:17). Clearly, this demonstrated that the nobleman (God) had anointed his servants (us) to take the money he had given them and to use it to make even more money.

> **God wants you to be blessed. He needs you to be prosperous to show others what kind of God we serve.**

When one of the master's servants hid his talent for fear of losing it, however, the nobleman chided him, saying, *"Why then did you not put my money in the bank, that at my coming I might have collected it with interest?"* (Luke 19:23). Here, Jesus was talking about business and about multiplying one's investment. He even implied that if you're not shrewd in business, you are at risk of losing any blessing from God. We have to get used to the fact that we have been anointed by God to make money.

[Jesus] *was rich, yet for your sakes He became poor, that you through His poverty might become rich.*

(2 Corinthians 8:9)

God wants you to be blessed. He needs you to be prosperous to show others what kind of God we serve. There has never been a better time to be blessed. God is raising up believers who will be blessed not only in finances, but also with influence over business, education, government, and all areas of society. Wall Street may fail. Washington, D.C., may fail. But God and His covenant of prosperity will never fail.

As we journey to the Promised Land, I can hear God begging us, as He did with the children of Israel as they left Egypt, "Please, don't start this end-time journey without the silver and the gold." God wants you to prosper because you are His child. God needs you to prosper so that you may *"go into all the world and preach the gospel to every creature"* (Mark 16:15). You need to realize that you have been anointed by God to make money. God wants to bless you greatly so that you can *be* a great blessing!

Breaking the Curse of Poverty

In this chapter, we are going to break the curse of lack, insufficiency, and poverty over your life, once and for all! We have been studying the children of Israel as they came out of the desert and entered into the Promised Land. You can experience the same kind of deliverance in your life. But, as we receive deliverance in the physical realm, we also need to receive deliverance in the spiritual realm. We need our minds to be renewed from that old, limited desert/poverty mind-set. We need to stretch our thinking, break free from small-mindedness, and develop a God-sized vision for our lives.

Breaking the curse of poverty is the topic I love to teach more than almost anything else. What does God's Word have to say about finances and prosperity? I've been in the ministry for over three decades, and, in that time, I've witnessed Christian prosperity teaching go in two directions: I've heard people claim that everything is about money, and I've also heard people say that prosperity is an evil, sinful word that shouldn't be discussed in church. I've decided that if God talks about finances and prosperity, then we also need to talk about them in the church and throughout the kingdom of God.

To begin, let's go back to Deuteronomy again.

> *Therefore you shall keep the commandments of the*
> *LORD your God, to walk in His ways and to fear Him.*
> *For the LORD your God is bringing you into a good land,*
> *a land of brooks of water, of fountains and springs,*
> *that flow out of valleys and hills; a land of wheat*
> *and barley, of vines and fig trees and pomegranates,*
> *a land of olive oil and honey; a land in which you*
> *will eat bread without scarcity, in which you will*
> *lack nothing.*   (Deuteronomy 8:6–9)

This land is not one in which you "just get by" but a land *"in which you will lack nothing."* God was bringing His people out of the desert. He wants to bring His people out of the desert in our day and time, too! The "desert" symbolizes the land of "just getting by." This is where most of the church is camped. We used to be in Egypt, where we were slaves. God delivered us and saved us, and now, we are on our way to the Promised Land. Until we get there, though, we're still in the desert, just barely getting by. While we're here in the desert, every once in a while, God opens a window and gives us manna or brings fresh water from out of a rock. We're content because our bills are paid, there's gas in our cars, and, every once in a while, we can squeeze in a vacation at a second-rate motel. That's life in the desert. But God is not talking about a land of just getting by; He is talking about a land that flows—and overflows—with milk and honey, a land in which we lack nothing. To get out of the desert, we are going to have to change the way we think.

When I first got saved, Tiz and I were taught that if we really loved God, we should have no desire to live well in this life. The only thing that mattered was going to heaven. On this earth, we're all just sojourners passing through. Thus, we shouldn't become attached to the things of this world. If you wanted to drive a nice car, if you wanted to live in a nice house, then you were considered to be a "city dweller" and not a "kingdom builder." Worldly concerns were considered ungodly things that only wasted God's money—money that should be spent only on the kingdom of God.

It took me fifteen years to realize that this was the doctrine of man, not the doctrine of God!

Let's take another look at the passage on tithing from Malachi:

> "Return to Me, and I will return to you," says the LORD of hosts. "But you said, 'In what way shall we return?' Will a man rob God? Yet you have robbed Me! But you say, 'In what way have we robbed You?' In tithes and offerings." (Malachi 3:7–8)

Tiz and I have never missed a tithe. And we don't simply tithe; we've always given a minimum of 20 percent. We've always known how to give, but we haven't always known how to receive. It took a while for us to fully understand the next part of Malachi, which says,

> "Bring all the tithes into the storehouse, that there may be food in My house, and try Me now in this," says the LORD of hosts, "if I will not open for you the windows of heaven and pour out for you such blessing that there will not be room enough to receive it....And all nations will call you blessed." (verses 10, 12)

Insisting that the Christian world should embrace poverty is a false teaching and a part of the curse. We've got to lose that kind of thinking. Nowhere in the Bible does it say that God wants you poor. Instead, my Bible says, *"Beloved, I pray that you may prosper in all things and be in health, just as your soul prospers"* (3 John 1:2). God says, in effect, "As your knowledge grows, I'm not only going to release healing on your life but incredible prosperity, as well!"

When we are in a continual state of financial struggle and cannot pay our bills, we are not being good witnesses of who our God is before the world. Our God is not poor! My Bible says, *"Give, and it will be given to you: good measure, pressed down, shaken together, and running over"* (Luke 6:38). Then, the entire world will call you blessed. You can pay your bills when God prospers your business and you have money in the bank. That is being a good witness for the Lord.

People who are hurting and struggling, people who are without hope, should be able to look at our lives and see the blessings of our God! They should see the tangible manifestation of the goodness of God in our lives. There should be evidence of the blessings of God that will draw the world to Him. When others look at our lives, they should be asking, "How is your car paid off?" "How were you able to pay off your mortgage?" "How come your bills are paid?"

Our response should be, "Because I'm a Christian! My God is a good God! My God is a Giver, not a taker! I have a covenant with my God. As I serve Him, He blesses me with overflow and abundance in every area of my life!" God wants your life to be a living testimony that will draw the world to Him.

> **People should see the tangible manifestation of the goodness of God in our lives. There should be evidence of the blessings of God that will draw the world to Him.**

Think about the enemy's strategy: a teaching that insists that Christians are supposed to be poor. As we try to tell the world that we have what they need, they look at our hopelessness and say, "No, thanks! We don't want what you've got! There's already plenty of poverty in our world!"

"And all nations will call you blessed." They will call us blessed because they will see all of God's blessings in our lives! Being poor is certainly no sin, but there's something wrong if we want to remain poor. We all have to start somewhere. Life is a continual journey. As the hymn proclaims, "From glory to glory, He's changing me." But, before we can move into the blessings of God, we need to break the curse of poverty.

We have to renew our minds, change our perceptions, throw out those old religious teachings of poverty, and learn what God says about finances. Poverty is part of the curse—a curse with a cause.

The Curse of Poverty

There are four possible reasons that curses come on your life: first, because of something you've done; second, because of something you've inherited or unknowingly brought into your home; third, because of something that someone else has done to you; and fourth, the most common reason, because the church at large is not living in the blessings of God. The majority of the Christian world embraces the curse of poverty. We've been taught that poverty and Christianity go hand in hand. That is a false teaching and a curse.

The Bible says our religious traditions can cancel out the Word of God in our lives.

> [You make] *the word of God of no effect through your tradition which you have handed down. And many such things you do.* (Mark 7:13)

In our case, there is one Scripture that has been misunderstood, thereby releasing a curse of poverty on the church and a ceiling of containment over the lives of believers. *"For you know the grace of our Lord Jesus Christ, that though He was rich, yet for your sakes He became poor, that you through His poverty might become rich"* (2 Corinthians 8:9).

Of course, we all want to be like Jesus. But many believe that if Jesus was poor, then they should also be poor. We've been taught to picture poor little baby Jesus, wrapped in rags, born in a lowly manger. We have been taught that Jesus' entire life was lived out in poverty and lack. We picture Jesus as a homeless wanderer in a tattered robe, begging for food.

What does the Bible mean when it says Jesus *"became poor"*? For thirty-five years, I've heard people say, "Oh no, Pastor

Larry. God doesn't want us to be financially rich. He wants us to be spiritually rich. This Scripture doesn't mean rich with money." Really? The Son of God, the King of Kings, the Lord of Lords, became spiritually poor so that we could become spiritually rich? That's not what it means. The apostle Paul was referring to money. He was referring to wealth. When the Bible says that Jesus became poor, it does not mean that He became a beggar. It means that Jesus became poor on earth, forfeiting the riches He had in heaven. Yes, we are to be rich spiritually, but we are also to be rich financially.

> **Our God is not a poor, poverty-stricken God. There is nothing poverty-minded about our God or about heaven!**

Let me show you a picture of heaven. In Revelation 21, it says, *"And he who talked with me had a gold reed to measure the city, its gates, and its wall"* (verse 15). Scripture speaks of a solid gold tape measure. We think we're something special if we've got a gold-plated ink pen. This guy had a solid gold tape measure! But there's more.

> *The construction of its wall was of jasper; and the city was pure gold, like clear glass. The foundations of the wall of the city were adorned with all kinds of precious stones: the first foundation was jasper, the second sapphire, the third chalcedony, the fourth emerald, the fifth sardonyx, the sixth sardius, the seventh chrysolite, the eighth beryl, the ninth topaz, the tenth chrysoprase, the eleventh jacinth, and the twelfth amethyst. The twelve gates were twelve pearls: each individual gate was of one pearl. And the street of the city was pure gold, like transparent glass.* (verses 18–21)

God has twelve gates made of pearl. Our God is not a poor God! You've got to get this poverty mind-set out of your head! You've got to get this religious curse out of your mind. Our God is not a poor, poverty-stricken God. There is nothing poverty-minded about our God or about heaven!

I was raised with poverty thinking and teachings. When Tiz and I were first married, we lived in a mobile home that was eight feet wide by thirty-two feet long. We were taught a sacrificial poverty doctrine. For years, we lived in either a mobile home or a small apartment. At that time in our lives, we were happy to live that way. We were taught and believed that it was our *"reasonable service"* (Romans 12:1), and that the things of this world didn't matter.

As the years went by, Tiz and I began to question whether this doctrine came from God or from man's religious teachings. We began to search the Word of God for ourselves, and He began to open our eyes to all that He intended for His children. He took us to Deuteronomy 28, where, for the first time in our Christian lives, we saw the covenant of blessing that He promised His people. We realized that God has always intended for His people to have dominion, authority, and influence in the world. As God's people, we are supposed to have the wealth of the world in our hands and to establish God's dominion on the earth. The Bible also tells us that our Father *"has pleasure in the prosperity of His servant"* (Psalm 35:27).

As our spiritual thinking expanded, so did our physical and financial worlds. We began to experience the blessings of God! We became blessed in order to be a blessing to others! (See Genesis 12:2.) As we saw in the first chapter, God's covenant in Deuteronomy 28:2 tells us that *"all these blessings shall come upon you and overtake you, because you obey the voice of the LORD your God."* He will make us *"the head and not the tail"* (verse 13). He will pour out His resources and abundance upon us. He will bless our families, our health, and our finances!

Since Tiz and I learned these things, our lives have never been the same. And what the Lord has done for us, we are committed to see Him doing for you, too!

We have to break the curse of poverty on our minds and in our lives. I remember the first time I heard a preacher talk on biblical prosperity. He was referring to when the prophet Isaiah *"saw the Lord sitting on a throne, high and lifted up, and the train of His robe filled the temple"* (Isaiah 6:1). I remember that preacher saying, "Our God is a snappy dresser!"

God is so rich that He paves the streets of heaven with gold. Our God has an abundance of wealth. And it is our Father's good pleasure to give us the kingdom. In fact, Jesus told us, *"When you pray, say: Our Father in heaven, hallowed be Your name. Your kingdom come. Your will be done on earth as it is in heaven"* (Luke 11:2).

When the Bible says Jesus became poor, it was only in comparison with all that He had in heaven, where the streets are made of gold. You hear that half the world is starving because there aren't enough resources. The problem is not inadequate resources. The problem is that great quantities of the world's wealth have been "stored up" by certain people. Because too many Christians are content to make the minimum wage working for somebody else, we've become used to "getting by." We need to break that religious curse and realize that Jesus became poor so that we could become rich. In fact, if I had all the wealth of the world, I would be a poor man compared with the wealth Jesus had in heaven. Jesus became poor comparatively so that you and I could become rich. But first, we've got to lose that poverty mentality. We've got to get rid of that religious curse that says it's bad or unspiritual to want to be blessed. On the contrary, the desire to be blessed *is* spiritual.

God's Economy

After the death of John the Baptist, Jesus retreated to a deserted place, only to discover that a huge crowd had followed Him. Jesus turned to His disciples and said, *"You give them something to eat"* (Luke 9:13). Most Christians miss the significance of the disciples' response: *"We have no more than five loaves and two fish, unless we go and buy food for all these people"* (verse 13). They *had* the money to buy food for the crowd.

Jesus was telling His disciples to buy food for all of the people to eat. The Bible records that *"there were about five thousand men"* (verse 14). Including the women and children, there could have been around eighteen thousand hungry people there that day. Feeding such a crowd with today's money, at $7 per person, would have meant a bill of around $126,000, not including tip. And yet, *"they all ate and were filled, and twelve baskets of the leftover fragments were taken up by them"* (Luke 9:17).

It may sound spiritual to preach poverty, but Jesus came with good news for the poor: God does not want His children to live in poverty. In Hebrew culture, one of the greatest insults to a father is for his son or daughter to reject a gift from him. For example, imagine if I offered to buy one of my children a car, and he or she said, "No, Dad, I couldn't accept it." First of all, this is probably a terrible illustration, because there's not a chance any of my kids would ever do that! But imagine God saying, "I want to open the windows of the kingdom of heaven and pour such a blessing into your life that all your bills will be paid,

> **Jesus came with good news for the poor: God does not want His children to live in poverty.**

your house will be paid off, your car will be paid off; in fact, everything will be paid in full. You will have so much that you will have more than enough to help others and finance My work on the earth. You will have so much that you'll have to figure out where to give it all!" Now, imagine that, in response to this, we turn to God and say, "No, thanks. We're fine." How much would this disappoint Him?

I understand poverty. I understand being barely able to get by. But our God is not called "El Get By." He's *El Shaddai*, our powerful God of more than enough. If we don't have that understanding firmly rooted in our minds, the Father will bring a blessing or an opportunity our way—perhaps a business deal or a job proposal—but we'll think, *I don't know if God wants me to have that.* When we think like that, we squelch the power of God the Father.

Consider the story of the prodigal son. (See Luke 15:11–32.) This is the story of the son of a wealthy father who rebelled and wasted everything he had before coming to his senses and realizing that even his father's servants had it better than he did. If it were up to religion, this story would end with the son returning to his father, who, upon hearing of his return, would refuse to see him, leaving him to starve in the wilderness for a period of time in order to make him pay for what he had done. But this is not what the father does. The father sees him coming and runs out to meet him. He puts a ring on his finger and a robe on his shoulders. Then, he orders the fatted calf butchered. He is so overjoyed at the return of his son that he gives him all the good stuff: the best food, the ring of authority, and the robe of royalty.

But the story isn't over. There is another son. When he hears the sounds of rejoicing in his father's house, he asks a servant what is happening. He can't relate to the father's house being full of joy. Something has to be wrong. When he sees his father fawning over the lost son, he protests, "But, Father, don't you know all of the things he has done? He certainly doesn't deserve all of these blessings!" The father's goodness must have been a foreign concept to the older son. Even though he had done everything right, he had missed the blessing.

I don't know about you, but I don't want God to give me what I deserve. I want God to give me what has already been paid for in full by the blood of Jesus Christ. And what did the father say to the other son? He said, *"Son, you are always with me, and all that I have is yours"* (Luke 15:31). Think about that. *"All that I have is yours."*

God's Good Pleasure

God wants you blessed for no other reason than the fact that He loves you. Your part of the bargain is simply to continue serving Him. You've got a call to change the world. You're to pay your tithes and give your offerings, and if you can do that, God wants you to be blessed—not someday but now.

Tiz and I had wanted for so long for our daughter Anna and her husband, Brandon, to have a baby. When their twins, Asher and Judah, were finally born, we were buying them trucks and baseball equipment and all sorts of toys before they could even roll over. Anna came to me and said, "Dad, don't buy all these things. The twins are so young; they can't even use their toys." Do you know why we, as grandparents, did that? Because it made us feel good.

God wants to do more than meet your need; He also wants to make you happy. *"It is the Father's good pleasure to give you the kingdom"* (Luke 12:32). Others will say, "Oh, no! You have to suffer, pay the price, and go without." All the while, God is trying to bless us, if we will just receive it.

Let me tell you about a couple who follow our ministry by watching the services we stream over the Internet. For two years, this couple had been partners with us, even though they had never physically attended a service! They had been Christians for thirty-five years, and, although they loved the Lord, they had struggled with depression and poverty all that time. Think of that—a child of God, saved and on the way to heaven, yet tormented by depression. Last year, they finally decided to join us in person for one of our Freedom Weekends, a time to celebrate having been delivered from the curses that bind. Recently, they wrote me to share that the past year had been like a "divine exchange." Filled with hope and peace after learning about the Jewish roots of our Christian faith, they have been touched with blessing after blessing. Their wealth has increased, their business has grown, their debts have been paid off, and they

> **God wants to do more than meet your need; He also wants to make you happy.**

no longer struggle with depression. They exchanged the fear and doubt that had controlled their lives for more of God's joy, blessings, and peace!

This couple experienced a major shift in their spirits and their thinking. I remember when I had to make a similar shift. While we were still in Portland, a businessman came up to me after I had finished preaching and said, "Pastor Larry, can my wife and I see you?" I said, "Well, sure." When we got to my office, the man said, "We came into the church a couple of months ago, and, since then, God has changed our lives, saved our marriage, and blessed our business. We just wanted to show you our appreciation."

In ministry, this is sometimes jokingly referred to as a "holy handshake." Somebody shakes your hand and, in so doing, transfers a buck into your hand from the palm of his hand. But this guy reached into his pocket, pulled out a set of keys, and tossed them to me. These weren't just any keys. They had a Mercedes-Benz emblem on them. I asked, "Brother, what's this?" He said, "Well, God told me to give you that new black Mercedes-Benz out there—the big one. The S500."

I'd love to tell you that I said, "Oh, praise God. Brother, I receive it. God bless you!" The truth is, I didn't take it. I didn't accept this man's gift because all I could think about was, *What will the people think?* So, I said no.

The next day, I was at a conference in Atlanta with several well-known church leaders. At that time, Tiz and I were the "new kids on the ministry block." We all went to lunch together, and, as we were talking, I mentioned being offered a car. Suddenly, there were responses all around the table. "Oh, man! Aren't those great cars?" "Doesn't it drive wonderfully?" "You'll feel so safe in that car." I had to tell them that I hadn't accepted the car because of what others might think. One of them said, "If they're the right kind of people, they'll think, *Praise God, I'm next!*"

I was stunned. I asked, "You mean that it's okay for me to have something like that?"

He said, "Brother, all the world wants to call you blessed. Don't you turn down that kind of blessing."

The next Sunday, I told the congregation to open their Bibles to Matthew 7:8: *"For everyone who asks receives, and he who seeks finds."* Then, I turned to the man who had offered me the car and asked, "Brother, you still got those car keys? Can you hook a brother up?" And God changed my life.

This year, God's ready to hook you up with His blessings if you're ready to receive them.

Possessing the Promised Land

Y ou've probably heard the popular saying "Money isn't every-thing." We all have. And, though it's true that money isn't *everything*, money *is* a very important something in the world in which we live. You've also heard the saying "Money won't buy you happiness." Again, while it is true that money, by itself, can't buy happiness, most people would agree that money does help. My happiness lies with my family, my friends, and my relationship with God. I feel as if I am the most blessed man on earth because of my wife, Tiz. We have been married for over thirty years. We have three beautiful children and, so far, three grandchildren, who are the loves of our lives. My oldest daughter is married to a great man who is also our church's worship leader. Our son has a beautiful wife who runs our children's ministry. We are all healthy. We love pastoring such great people here in Dallas. Our television program is exploding all over the world. Life is great!

But you know what? Having extra money at the end of the month makes our lives better, and it will make your life better, too.

Look at what God's Word says in Ecclesiastes 10:19: *"A feast is made for laughter, and wine makes merry; but money answers everything."* What does God mean when He tells us *"money answers everything"*? It's simple. Money buys your house. Money buys your food. Money supports the church, television programs, and missions. Money also allows you to go on vacation, buy birthday presents, purchase new clothes, and drive new cars. Money gives us the freedom not only to be blessed but also to be a blessing to others. *"Money answers everything"* that God puts in our hearts to do. While we all agree that money isn't everything, let's not underestimate the power of money. I remember the words of the character Tevye in the musical *Fiddler on the Roof.* As he is about to sing the song, "If I Were a Rich Man," he says, "It's no shame to be poor, but it's no great honor either."

God wants to put money into your hands. You may wonder, *Pastor Larry, how do you know this?* It's in God's Word. The Bible tells us that, in the very last days, there will be a great end-time transfer of wealth.

> *A good man leaves an inheritance for his children's children, but a sinner's wealth is stored up for the righteous.* (Proverbs 13:22 NIV)

> *Your gates will always stand open, they will never be shut, day or night, so that men may bring you the wealth of the nations.* (Isaiah 60:11 NIV)

> *You will feed on the wealth of nations, and in their riches you will boast.* (Isaiah 61:6 NIV)

> *I will extend peace to her like a river, and the wealth of nations like a flooding stream.* (Isaiah 66:12 NIV)

The Bible warns us to beware the strategies of the devil. The trick he has used on the church for centuries is telling us that to be really spiritual, we need to be poor. By knowing what God's Word says about money, we can destroy Satan's argument and break the curse of poverty by the blood of Jesus and the crown of thorns. But the enemy has another strategy, one he uses more frequently than the first. It's called the "spirit of containment."

The Spirit of Containment

I want you to think about four things: Israel, Egypt, the desert, and the Promised Land. When the Word of God tells us about Egypt, it is not just a history lesson about God's people coming home; it's also an illustration of the promises of God for all of us. Israel represents you. Egypt represents the world before you met the Lord. In Egypt—the world—we were slaves to harsh taskmasters. As slaves, the Israelites ate a basic diet of onions, garlic, and bread, and, occasionally, a little meat or fish. (See Numbers 11:5.) As a slave, it was barely enough to exist.

When God's people left Egypt, their journey led them into the wilderness. No longer did they depend on the world—the Egyptians—to give them their small portions. Now, they depended on God—*Jehovah Jireh*—to be their Provider.

> *Then the LORD said to Moses, "Behold, I will rain bread from heaven for you."* (Exodus 16:4)

> *And when the layer of dew lifted, there, on the surface of the wilderness, was a small round substance, as fine as frost on the ground. So when the children of Israel saw it, they said to one another, "What is it?" For they did not know what it was. And Moses said to them, "This is the bread which the LORD has given you to eat."* (verses 14–15)

What an amazing thing! God was proving to His people that He was their provider. In Egypt, they were slaves and received only leftovers. Now, each day, God was giving them enough to last them until the next day. As great as this was, meeting His people's daily needs is not God's ultimate goal—not for Israel back then, and not for you today. Egypt was "the land of not enough." The wilderness was "the land of just enough."

But God has a Promised Land, "the land of more than enough," a land flowing with milk and honey.

> *Go up to a land flowing with milk and honey; for I will not go up in your midst, lest I consume you on the way, for you are a stiff-necked people.*   (Exodus 33:3)

> *And the* Lord *said: "I have surely seen the oppression of My people who are in Egypt, and have heard their cry because of their taskmasters, for I know their sorrows. So I have come down to deliver them out of the hand of the Egyptians, and to bring them up from that land to a good and large land, to a land flowing with milk and honey, to the place of the Canaanites and the Hittites and the Amorites and the Perizzites and the Hivites and the Jebusites."*   (Exodus 3:7–8)

> *For the* Lord *your God is bringing you into a good land, a land of brooks of water, of fountains and springs, that flow out of valleys and hills; a land of wheat and barley, of vines and fig trees and pomegranates, a land of olive oil and honey; a land in which you will eat bread without scarcity, in which you will lack nothing; a land whose stones are iron and out of whose hills you can dig copper. When you have eaten and are full, then you shall bless the* Lord *your God for the good land which He has given you.* (Deuteronomy 8:7–10)

God is teaching us that *He* is our Provider, not the world. He is showing us that, no matter how hard or impossible it may seem, *He* is the same yesterday, today, and tomorrow (see Hebrews 13:8), *He* will bring water out of a rock (see Exodus 17:6), and *He* will rain our daily food down from heaven (see Exodus 16:4). But we must not stop. If you are passing through a desert place—with emphasis on *passing through*—God will bring you a miracle. His plan was never for His people to remain in the wilderness. They are to pass through the desert on their way—on *your* way—to the Promised Land.

Look at the description of that land again: a land *flowing* with milk and honey; a land of brooks, fountains, and springs that *flow* out of valleys and hills. What a contrast with the desert. I've been in that desert many times. There is no water. Nothing grows. God wants us to know that He can cause a rock to produce water when we need a miracle. But He doesn't want us depending on a miracle in order to make it one more day or one more month. No, He wants us to live in a land that is flowing constantly with His blessings; a land of wheat and barley, of vines and fig trees; a land in which we will lack nothing. We are out of Egypt. Now, God is taking us through the wilderness and into the Promised Land. He's taking us from "the land of not enough," through "the land of just enough," and into "the land of more than enough"— a land flowing with all the promises of God.

> **God is taking us through the wilderness and into the Promised Land. He's taking us from "the land of not enough," through "the land of just enough," and into "the land of more than enough."**

I recently heard a rabbinical teaching in which someone asked God, "Lord, why don't I get my prayers answered?" The Lord replied, "Because you ask for too little." The rabbi then gave the following illustration: we are praying for a one-pound miracle, but God has a one-hundred-pound miracle that He wants to give us. In other words, God's answer is too big to fit within our small prayers. We need to think bigger!

> *...lest; when you have eaten and are full, and have built beautiful houses and dwell in them....*
>
> (Deuteronomy 8:12)

Notice that God's Word says *"houses"*—more than one house. Why is this significant? One answer is found in Deuteronomy 28:12, where God tells us that His children will be the lenders, not the borrowers. God wants you to own your house, as well as other houses, buildings, and real estate, so that other people will rent from you. Think bigger!

> *The LORD will open to you His good treasure, the heavens, to give the rain to your land in its season, and to bless all the work of your hand. You shall lend to many nations, but you shall not borrow. And the LORD will make you the head and not the tail; you shall be above only, and not be beneath, if you heed the commandments of the LORD your God, which I command you today, and are careful to observe them. And the LORD will make you the head and not the tail; you shall be above only, and not be beneath, if you heed the commandments of the LORD your God, which I command you today, and are careful to observe them.*
>
> (Deuteronomy 28:12–13)

What does this mean for you? I have a saying I teach wherever I go: "Somebody is going to get blessed; it might as well be me. In your workplace, somebody is going to get a raise or a promotion; it might as well be you." Tiz and I hear it all the time. Our congregants say, "Pastor, they laid a bunch of people off at work, but my boss called me in, and, instead of being laid off, I got a raise." Think about what God's Word says about you: you are to be the *"head and not the tail."* You are to be *"above only, and not beneath."* Did you see that word *"only"*? No more valleys and no more wilderness. God's Word on you is *"above only, and not beneath."* Think bigger. Can I take you one more step into your God-given Promised Land?

> *The LORD will grant you plenty of goods, in the fruit of your body, in the increase of your livestock, and in the produce of your ground, in the land of which the LORD swore to your fathers to give you.*
>
> (Deuteronomy 28:11)

...and when your herds and your flocks multiply, and your silver and your gold are multiplied, and all that you have is multiplied.... (Deuteronomy 8:13)

As I'm writing these words, I feel a spirit of prophecy on me, being passed on to you. When God says that *"your herds and your flocks"* will multiply, He is talking about your business. A great place to start is by saying, "Lord, I need a job." Then, begin to think bigger: "Lord, I need a raise." Then, think bigger: "Lord, I want to be the boss." Now, we're getting to the Promised Land. Think even bigger: "Lord, I want to own my own business."

You may be thinking, *Pastor Larry, could God really do that for me?* Look again at Deuteronomy 8:13. God said that *your* herds and *your* flocks will multiply. Not somebody else's but *yours.* Look at the next few words: *"**Your** silver and **your** gold are multiplied."* Wow! Now we are talking about a Promised Land that is *flowing* the way God said it would in these last days.

Let me show you something that will help you to think bigger. Financial experts say that more than 80 percent of the millionaires in America are *new* millionaires. That means they are self-made and did not inherit their money. Romans 2:11 reminds us that *"there is no partiality with God."* Therefore, if *they* can do it, *you* can do it. It doesn't matter if you are young or old, male or female, white, black, brown, or anything else. The Word of God is the will of God for your life.

Let me give a prophetic word to those of you who already own your own business. You are about to see God's blessings multiplied on your life. Look at Deuteronomy 28 once again:

The LORD will command the blessing on you in your storehouses and in all to which you set your hand, and He will bless you in the land which the LORD your God is giving you....And the LORD will grant you plenty of goods, in the fruit of your body, in the increase of your livestock, and in the produce of your ground, in the land of which the LORD swore to your fathers to give you. The LORD will open to you His good treasure, the heavens, to give the rain to your land in its season, and to bless all the work of your hand. You shall lend to many nations, but you shall not borrow.

(Deuteronomy 28:8, 11–12)

God will bless everything to which you set your hands. He will grant you *"plenty of goods"* and *"increase."* These words have never been truer. Now is the greatest time in history for God to put the wealth of Egypt—the world's wealth—into your hands. It's happening right now, all over the world. God's people are experiencing amazing blessings. Now, it's your turn!

Look at Deuteronomy 8:18: *"And you shall remember the LORD your God, for it is He who gives you power to get wealth."* This is one of the greatest teachings in the Word of God. God says, in effect, "I give you *power* to go out there and get wealth—to enter into the Promised Land, flowing with milk and honey. It's there. Go get it! And, when you do, I'll give you the power from heaven to do it. You may have to kill a few 'giants,' but I will give you the power to do that, too."

For the LORD your God is bringing you into a good land, a land of brooks of water, of fountains and springs, that flow out of valleys and hills; a land of wheat and barley, of vines and fig trees and pomegranates, a land of olive oil and honey; a land in which you will eat bread without scarcity, in which you will lack nothing; a land whose stones are iron and out of whose hills you can dig copper. (Deuteronomy 8:7–9)

This is God's promise to you. It's a land that *flows*; it doesn't trickle. It's a land in which you will lack nothing. It's not a land of "barely getting by" or a land of "meeting only your most basic needs." No, a Promised Land is where you and your family lack nothing. It's a land of abundance, a land where you don't just have a roof over your heads but where you have *beautiful* houses. And you're the ones who own them!

Then, God says, *"And when your herds and your flocks multiply, and your silver and your gold are multiplied, and all that you have is multiplied..."* (Deuteronomy 8:13). He will multiply all you have. What an awesome God we serve!

> **A Promised Land is where you and your family lack nothing. It's a land of abundance, a land where you don't just have a roof over your heads but where you have beautiful houses.**

But I have to show you one more thing to make this teaching clear.

> *When you have eaten and are full, then you shall bless the LORD your God for the good land which He has given you. Beware that you do not forget the LORD your God by not keeping His commandments, His judgments, and His statutes which I command you today....Then you say in your heart, "My power and the might of my hand have gained me this wealth."*
>
> (verses 10–11, 17)

Let me explain what this means. First, God is not telling us that these blessing are bad or wrong. They can't be. Remember, it is God who gives us power to gain wealth. Instead, God is reminding us that all our blessings come from Him, and we must not forget that.

> *And you shall remember the LORD your God, for it is He who gives you power to get wealth.* (verse 18)

Second, now that you are blessed, don't stop serving God.

> *You shall keep the commandments of the LORD your God, to walk in His ways and to fear Him.* (verse 6)

And Deuteronomy 8:11:

Beware that you do not forget the LORD *your God by not keeping His commandments, His judgments, and His statutes which I command you today.*

I've been in the ministry for a long time. I've seen people stop serving the Lord because of battles they were going through. But I've also seen people who started serving the Lord with nothing. As they obeyed and believed in God's Word and His promises, the blessings began to flow. To most people, this blessing increases their service to God and His kingdom. But, every once in a while, God's blessings have the opposite result. This is when He says, in effect, "I've brought you out of Egypt—'the land of not enough.' I've brought you out of the desert—'the land of just enough.' But now, I'm bringing you into the Promised Land—'the land of more than enough.'" Think about that. The blessing and abundance of God are going to be so great on your life that He has to give you a warning. You are going to be so blessed that you will be tempted to forget that it was God who gave you the power to gain all that wealth.

As I'm closing this chapter, I feel in my spirit that I am with you personally, wherever you are. And the Lord has said to me, *Larry, those who are reading these words will not fail.* Wow! God said *you* will not fail. He is asking me to tell you that He is going to bless you so greatly that what you will accomplish through His anointing will help bring the Messiah back to Jerusalem. The world will call you blessed. The blessing and the favor of God that are being released into your life right now will be a witness to your family and friends of the goodness of God. God wants you to know: "You have been faithful with little. Now, get ready. You are leaving the wilderness, and, today, *you* are entering into the land *flowing* with milk and honey." As I am writing this, God's Spirit is flowing through me, and He is saying to you, "Welcome to the Promised Land."

Enjoy the journey. It's going to be more exciting than you ever dreamed. He *"is able to do exceedingly abundantly above all that we ask or think"* (Ephesians 3:20)! So, *think big!*

7

The Miraculous Blessing of the Firstfruits Offering

One of the most exciting promises God gives us is found in Malachi, where He says that if we return to Him, He will open the windows of heaven over us and pour out for us such a blessing that we won't have enough room to hold it all. (See Malachi 3:10.) How many of us have prayed, "Lord, open up Your windows of heaven over me," but it never seems to happen in the fullness we are looking for? We may receive a small blessing here or there but not the open-window type of blessing we read about God having for us. What's wrong? What is keeping those windows of God's prosperity and abundance closed? What is it going to take to unstick those heavenly windows and get them to open wide?

Remember what the Lord told us in Hosea 4:6: *"My people are destroyed for lack of knowledge."* God wants to show you the truth that will set you and your finances free. The secret to the windows of heaven found in Malachi 3 is hidden at the very end of verse 8, where God says, *"In tithes and offerings."*

At this point, you're probably thinking, *Pastor Larry, I've heard this before. I've given my tithe, and I usually add an offering to it, but the windows of heaven still do not open.*

Have patience. I am about to reveal the secret to the end-time prosperity God wants to bring, not only to the church but also to your life. The truth you are about to learn will finally set you financially free.

Most of us know what is meant when God speaks of the *tithe*. It means that 10 percent of what we earn belongs to God. But what does God mean when He says, "Not only does the tithe belong to Me, but the offering does, as well"? It's a biblical mystery that will open *"the windows of heaven,"* and it happens three times each year.

> *"And try Me now in this," says the* Lord *of hosts, "if I will not open for you the windows of heaven and pour out for you such blessing that there will not be room enough to receive it."*   (Malachi 3:10)

One of the greatest secrets God is unveiling in these last days has to do with the biblical holidays, or feasts, that are found in the Old Testament. There are many hidden truths that God wants us to know, truths that may be understood only by reading and studying the Bible with a Jewish, or Hebrew, mind-set. God is providing the keys of the Christian church as He reveals His plans through celebrations such as Passover, Pentecost, and Sukkot, or the Feast of Tabernacles.

> *And the* Lord *spoke to Moses, saying, "Speak to the children of Israel, and say to them: 'The feasts of the* Lord, *which you shall proclaim to be holy convocations, these are My feasts.'"*   (Leviticus 23:1–2)

The Hebrew word translated as *"feasts"* means "appointed time." God told Moses to explain to the people that these feasts of the Lord were appointed times—special appointments with Him to receive revelation and experience blessing. God was saying, in effect, "I am going to reserve specific dates on My calendar for you to reconnect with Me and with My plans to bless you spiritually, physically, and financially."

I know that many of you believe that these Old Testament teachings are no longer needed in Christianity today. But remember that Jesus said, *"Do not think that I came to destroy the Law or the Prophets. I did not come to destroy but to fulfill"* (Matthew 5:17). In other words, Jesus was saying, "I didn't come to do away with the Torah, or the law, but to show you how to live it, thereby releasing God's power and blessing into your lives."

> **God's Word is not meant to bind us in legalism but to put us on a path that will guide us to all the blessings God has for us.**

It's important to understand that we are not talking about legalism. We're talking about the Torah as a revelation that connects us to God's blessings. Jesus continued, *"For assuredly, I say to you, till heaven and earth pass away, one jot or one tittle will by no means pass from the law till all is fulfilled"* (verse 18).

When we see the word *law*, it can mean two things. In Greek, it means *legalism*—the dos and don'ts of religion that we must adhere to in order to be "saved" and get to heaven. But in Hebrew, God's law refers to a "pathway" or "teaching." Our guide, God's Word, is not meant to bind us in legalism but to put us on a path that will lead us to all the blessings God has for us, as well as to show us how to live beneath the open windows of heaven.

Let me give you an example. If you live in the United States, you know that we Americans celebrate certain holidays to honor our nation and its people. On the Fourth of July, or Independence Day, we celebrate our country's freedom. In November, we celebrate Veterans Day to honor the men and women who served in wartime. Does celebrating the Fourth of July or Veterans Day make someone an American? Of course not. Does celebrating these holidays teach our children what it means to appreciate freedom and honor those who made it possible? Does it make us better Americans? I'd say it does. This is what God's laws, or pathways and guides, do for us.

Let's look at a few teachings from God's Word that, at first glance, may seem to contradict one another.

Saved by Grace...

For by grace you have been saved through faith, and that not of yourselves; it is the gift of God, not of works, lest anyone should boast. (Ephesians 2:8–9)

Therefore by the deeds of the law no flesh will be justified in His sight, for by the law is the knowledge of sin....Therefore we conclude that a man is justified by faith apart from the deeds of the law.

(Romans 3:20, 28)

Saved by Works...

You see then that a man is justified by works, and not by faith only. (James 2:24)

Now behold, one came and said to [Jesus], "Good Teacher, what good thing shall I do that I may have eternal life?" So He said to him, "Why do you call Me good? No one is good but One, that is, God. But if you want to enter into life, keep the commandments."

(Matthew 19:16–17)

Let me explain the difference between these sets of verses. We are saved by God's grace. Period. We are saved by nothing else! But, once we are saved, God's Word teaches us how to live our lives here on earth, how to walk and act like the children of God. It also guides us into experiencing all the blessings that God has for us.

Let me ask another question. Do you have to tithe in order to be a Christian? We know that God says, in effect, "A tenth is Mine." But does obeying God's Word and giving 10 percent make us Christians? Your answer is, I hope, "Of course not!" But let's ask another question: Would obeying God's Word by giving 10 percent make us *better* Christians? The answer is yes. Why? First, because God says to do so, and it is right to obey Him. Second, when we give of our wealth, God's house can be full, and His church can afford to spread the news of His love. Third, it is the first step to living under the open windows of heaven.

You see, obeying God's laws is not about legalism; it's about staying on the pathway to God's blessings.

In Malachi 3, the Lord is reaching out to us, saying, *"Return to Me, and I will return to you"* (verse 7). I can see the Lord saying, in effect, "Please, return to Me. I want to take care of you. I want to bless you. I want to open My windows of heaven and pour out for you such a blessing." We look back at Him with eyes wide open, an expression of hope. We have so many needs. We respond with excitement. *"In what way shall we return?"* (verse 7). And God answers, "As I taught your fathers before you: *'In tithes and offerings'* (verse 8). Return to Me in this way, *'as in the days of old, as in former years'* (verse 4)."

> **Obeying God's laws is not about legalism; it's about staying on the pathway to God's blessings.**

In Malachi, the Lord is speaking to Jewish people. Now, through Jesus, you and I have been included, "grafted in" with Israel. The Jewish people understood what God meant. They understood what the offering was all about. The offering was the key. The offering was the secret. Even now, the offering, as in the days of old, is the mystery that Jesus meant by the thirty-, sixty-, and hundredfold blessing. The offering is the miracle that will open the windows of heaven. Once you see this, each window—there are three of them—will open. And after they open, they will never close again. But, before He opens the windows of heaven, God must *open our eyes*.

> *Three times a year all your males shall appear before the LORD your God in the place which He chooses: at the Feast of Unleavened Bread, at the Feast of Weeks,*

*and at the Feast of Tabernacles; and they shall not
appear before the LORD empty-handed.*

(Deuteronomy 16:16)

According to ancient Jewish wisdom, three times each
year, God brings a special window from heaven that passes
over us. The Hebrew word for *"window,"* as found in Malachi
3:10, means a "portal" or "chimney." It signifies God's ability to
meet your needs as each window passes over you. This happens
three times a year: on Passover, on Shavuot, and on Sukkot,
or the Feast of Tabernacles. This is exactly what the Lord has
wanted to show us in the last days. This is the revelation we
have been waiting for.

*You shall know the truth, and the truth shall make you
free.*   (John 8:32)

Remember, it's the truth we know—the truth we understand—that will set us free. Three times a year, God sends an
opportunity to receive a miracle. Three times a year, He says, in
effect, "Come before Me, but don't come *"empty-handed."* This is
the key to the windows of heaven. If we don't know about these
special offerings, they will pass us by, and we will wonder why
the windows of heaven won't open.

You're probably wondering, *Pastor Larry, would God really
pass us by if we didn't know about this?* Look at this amazing
example we have in the Bible about Jesus and a man. Although
the account is found in three of the four gospels, only in Mark do
we learn that the man was *"blind Bartimaeus, the son of Timaeus"*
(Mark 10:46). But I want you to read the account in Luke:

*Then it happened, as He was coming near Jericho, that
a certain blind man sat by the road begging. And hearing a multitude passing by, he asked what it meant. So
they told him that Jesus of Nazareth was passing by.
And he cried out, saying, "Jesus, Son of David, have
mercy on me!" Then those who went before warned*

him that he should be quiet; but he cried out all the more, "Son of David, have mercy on me!" So Jesus stood still and commanded him to be brought to Him. And when he had come near, He asked him, saying, "What do you want Me to do for you?" He said, "Lord, that I may receive my sight." Then Jesus said to him, "Receive your sight; your faith has made you well."

(Luke 18:35–42)

What a great teaching on God's love and power. But notice that Bartimaeus heard *"a multitude passing by"* him. Some in the crowd *"told him that Jesus of Nazareth was passing by."* Did you see that? Jesus was *"passing by"* him, even though He wanted to heal Bartimaeus, was able to heal him, and, inevitably, would heal him. Jesus was Bartimaeus' window of heaven, but He was passing by and, according to Scripture, would never return to Jericho during His short time left on earth.

This is what happens for us, three times each year. When we seize these special times, Jesus stops and opens the windows of heaven, saying, as He did to Bartimaeus, "Receive your blessing. Your faith has made you well."

This is what God will do for you. Deuteronomy 16:16 says, *"Three times a year all your males shall appear before the LORD... and they shall not appear before the LORD empty-handed."* We are to bring a special offering, a "firstfruits offering," to make sure the windows of heaven do not pass us by.

Once again, anytime we give to God, He will bless us. But these times are different. These times are special. Each of these offerings produces a particular harvest, or blessing, that is released from heaven to cover you and your family for the entire year.

Let's briefly discuss the blessings that are released when we give a firstfruits offering *"as in the days of old"* (Malachi 3:4).

The Passover Offering

According to ancient Jewish wisdom, there are three things that, according to God, have no limits. The first is the corner of the field from which the poor can glean the leftover harvest. The second is the studying of the Torah, God's Word. And the third is the firstfruits offering. What that means to us is that there's no limit to the goodness and generosity of God. There are no limits to the endless revelations in God's Word, and there are no limits to the incredible blessings that are released by our firstfruits offerings.

> **There are no limits to the endless revelations in God's Word, and there are no limits to the incredible blessings that are released by our firstfruits offerings.**

The first of the offerings in Deuteronomy 16:16 is the Passover offering. On the second day of Passover is the Feast of Unleavened Bread. This is an offering to God that produces three different, distinct blessings in your life. We need to remember that when God sent Moses to bring His people out of Egypt, for the most part, they were no longer serving the God of Abraham, Isaac, and Jacob. Many of them had turned to the gods of Egypt. They had forgotten their God and had begun to model the lifestyle of their captors. God saved them from the Egyptians, not because they deserved it but because of His grace. It's the same with you and me. God has saved us, not because we deserve it but because of His grace.

A Divine Measure of Grace

Grace is simply the undeserved, unmerited, unlimited favor of God. Out of His grace, God not only answered the prayers of His people but also did much more. When the first nine plagues hit Egypt, among the things destroyed were all the crops in the fields. The plagues of hail and locusts wiped out the barley all across Egypt, except in the area of Goshen, where the children of God lived.

So there was hail, and fire mingled with the hail, so very heavy that there was none like it in all the land of Egypt since it became a nation. And the hail struck throughout the whole land of Egypt, all that was in the field, both man and beast; and the hail struck every herb of the field and broke every tree of the field....Now the flax and the barley were struck, for the barley was in the head and the flax was in bud. But the wheat and the spelt were not struck, for they are late crops.
(Exodus 9:24–25, 31–32)

God later said, *"The first of the firstfruits of your land you shall bring into the house of the LORD your God"* (Exodus 23:19). After God had, by grace, spared their crops, spared their livestock, and delivered them from the bondage of Egypt, He instructed them that, each year, they were to bring Him an offering of the firstfruits of their harvest.

Speak to the children of Israel, and say to them: "When you come into the land which I give to you, and reap its harvest, then you shall bring a sheaf of the firstfruits of your harvest to the priest. He shall wave the sheaf before the Lord, to be accepted on your behalf; on the day after the Sabbath the priest shall wave it. And you shall offer on that day, when you wave the sheaf, a male lamb of the first year, without blemish, as a burnt offering to the Lord. Its grain offering shall be two-tenths of an ephah of fine flour mixed with oil, an offering made by fire to the Lord, for a sweet aroma; and its drink offering shall be of wine, one-fourth of a hin. You shall eat neither bread nor parched grain nor fresh grain until the same day that you have brought an offering to your God; it shall be a statute forever throughout your generations in all your dwellings."
(Leviticus 23:10–14)

There are two main reasons for this barley offering: first, to receive the same needed grace in our lives that Israel needed in Egypt, and, second, to remind us that because of God's grace, we are not poor, nor are we slaves to the world. By His grace, we, the children of God, are free. *"Therefore if the Son makes you free, you shall be free indeed"* (John 8:36). When we come before the Lord with this first of the year's three special offerings, He opens the first window of heaven and releases over our lives the first blessing of grace, the favor of God, for an entire year.

Divine Protection

The second blessing released by our Passover offering is divine protection. We have already seen how God protected Israel when the first nine plagues were released. The Egyptians' crops and cattle were destroyed, while the children of God, who lived in Goshen, were spared. For the Egyptians, their livelihoods were wiped out.

> **God has a plan of divine protection for you and me. Just as He protected His children in Egypt, He will protect us when we bring our Passover offering.**

It's hard not to relate this to our world today. In the realm of finances, history seems to be repeating itself. So many people around the world have experienced dire losses as the stock market has plunged, banks have failed, and the housing market has collapsed. But God has a plan of divine protection for you and me. Just as He protected His children in Egypt, He will protect us when we bring our Passover offering each year. We have seen the grace of God and His divine protection over His children with the first nine plagues. But that doesn't even compare with His divine protection when the tenth and final plague passed through the land:

> *Now the blood shall be a sign for you on the houses where you are. And when I see the blood, I will pass over you; and the plague shall not be on you to destroy* ***you*** *when I strike the land of Egypt....And it came to pass at midnight that the LORD struck all the firstborn*

*in the land of Egypt, from the firstborn of Pharaoh who
sat on his throne, to the firstborn of the captive who
was in the dungeon, and all the firstborn of livestock.*
(Exodus 12:13, 29, emphasis added)

The tenth plague that passed through Egypt struck down
the firstborn, or firstfruit, of every family. To that point, previous plagues had targeted only crops, water, and livestock. Now,
the threat was to the firstfruit of every home. God, therefore,
told each household of the children of Israel to sacrifice a lamb
and to apply the blood of the lamb to the doorposts of its home.

In the Bible, the final *"you"* in verse 13 is italicized. For the
sake of this book, it is in bold type. When a word in the Bible is
italicized, it means that it was not in the original text but was
added later for clarity. So, let's read this verse the way it originally appeared in the Torah: "And when I see the blood, I will
pass over you; and the plague shall not be on you to destroy."
Ancient Jewish wisdom teaches that when you apply the blood
on your doorposts, not only will the destroyer be unable to strike
you, but he will not be allowed to touch anyone *under your roof.*

When we bring the firstfruits offering to God, it protects
our children through the blood of the Lamb, just as it protected
all of the Israelites' children that night in Egypt. It releases
the divine protection of the blood of the Lamb on you and all
of your household: your spouse, your children, your children's
spouses, and your grandchildren.

When we bring the firstfruits offering to God, we place
our entire households under His grace and protection. Every
spouse, every child, and every in-law is saved when a man
applies the blood to his doorposts.

*For the unbelieving husband is sanctified by the wife,
and the unbelieving wife is sanctified by the husband;
otherwise your children would be unclean, but now
they are holy.* (1 Corinthians 7:14)

I'm not saying that the lost don't need Jesus; I am saying there is an angel of protection, a covering of the blood, and an umbrella of grace that rest upon all the members of your family, refusing to allow the destroyer to get them. You and your family will be saved by grace. This is part of the covenant we have with God and part of the unlimited, undeserved, unmerited blessing we enter into when we sow our firstfruits offering.

Divine Favor

The third blessing is favor with our fellow man and woman.

Now the children of Israel had done according to the word of Moses, and they had asked from the Egyptians articles of silver, articles of gold, and clothing. And the Lord *had given the people favor in the sight of the Egyptians, so that they granted them what they requested. Thus they plundered the Egyptians.*

(Exodus 12:35–36)

> **Without God, you are limited to what man can do, but with God, you have favor in the eyes of other people.**

When the Israelites left, they found favor in the eyes of the Egyptians, who gave them their silver, gold, and clothing. This is important because even though we need favor from God to see the blessing, we also need God to give us favor with our fellow man. Once again, wealth is an equal part of your redemption. This goes along with Luke 6:38, which promises that God's blessings *"will be put into your bosom."* The King James Version says, *"...shall men give into your bosom."*

During Passover, the Israelites were to sow a firstfruits offering of barley. As the food of animals and slaves, it was the least that their oppressors could spare. Proverbs says, *"The blessing of the* Lord *makes one rich, and He adds no sorrow with it"* (verse 10:22). In other words, without God, you are limited to what man can do, but with God, you have favor in the eyes of other people.

Finding favor with man means that God will speak to your boss and ask him or her to give you a raise. In your business, God will give you favor with the right clients. He will give you favor when you are considering an investment. Your employer will say, "I don't know why I'm doing this, because I need to lay off twenty people, but I'm doubling your income." That's the type of favor that God gives us with man.

The Passover firstfruits offering releases the thirtyfold blessing into our lives for the entire year.

A Testimony of the Firstfruits Offering

Let me tell you Lynn's story. Even though she had attended a Bible college and was serving at her church four days a week, she knew something was missing in her faith. Crying out to God one day, she saw one of our television programs, on which I was teaching about the feast of Passover. That program started Lynn on a journey that altered the course of her life. Hungry for more, she visited a messianic church in her area, trying to capture what she had heard me teaching that day. Eventually, she found our services on the Internet, which brought the fulfillment she had been looking for. Imagine spending all those years in Bible college and serving at her church, knowing all the while that God had more for her life. In 2008, Lynn started her own business, but she didn't experience a substantial increase until she started giving firstfruit offerings and putting into practice the teachings she had learned from us. Since then, her income has nearly tripled, and she has needed to expand her office space due to the growth of her business. Lynn says it is interesting to see new clients seeking out her business because they learned about it by word of mouth. She knows this blessing is from God. One of her clients even donated five thousand dollars' worth of equipment that she desperately needed to accomplish this new expansion. Her business has been voted the best business in the county for two years in a row! Because the income from her two rental properties pays her bills and expenses, and the profits from her business paid for the expansion, she is now free and clear of debt. She flies to Dallas once a month just to join our church in person and to be under the anointing and worship there. Although she still lives on the East Coast, Lynn considers our church to be her church home. Her prayer now is to be able to move to Dallas and continue on the pathway of blessings that God has provided.

The Pentecost Offering

While the Passover offering gives us financial favor with man, the Pentecost—or *Shavuot*—offering gives us financial favor with God. Instead of barley, the Pentecost offering was one of wheat. Wheat represents people and prosperity. With it, God is saying, in effect, "Your prosperity is no longer by slavery or by what man will give you. Now, I will become *Jehovah Jireh*, your Provider." This offering connects us with God's supernatural favor, help, and equipping. It connects us with His unlimited supply of resources and provision!

While the barley offering was to remind Israel that, because of God, they were no longer slaves but had favor with man, the wheat offering was to signify that Israel had favor with both man *and* God. If we miss the Passover offering, we miss unmerited grace, divine protection, and the favor of our fellow man. If we miss the Pentecost offering, we miss supernatural favor from God. With this offering, we move from the thirtyfold to the sixtyfold blessing of God.

The Sukkot Offering

The last of the three yearly offerings brings us to the hundredfold blessing. This is the offering of Sukkot, also called the Feast of Tabernacles. With this offering, God brings in the "early rain" and the "latter rain." The early rain ensures that your harvest will take deep root; the latter rain ensures that your harvest will produce an abundance of fruit. Without the early rain, your root system will remain shallow, and the storms of life will wash away your harvest. But when you give the Sukkot offering, you activate the final part of Malachi 3:11: *"I will rebuke the devourer for your sakes, so that he will not destroy the fruit of your ground, nor shall the vine fail to bear fruit for you in the field."*

With these three offerings, we have favor with man, favor with God, and the promise that our harvests will root deeply and produce an abundance of fruit. We will not go through those valleys of darkness anymore. This offering brings us God's hundredfold blessing for the entire year!

> **With these three offerings, we have favor with man, favor with God, and the promise that our harvests will root deeply and produce an abundance of fruit.**

Let me share the story of one Sukkot offering miracle.

In 2008, my wife lost her job. This was heartbreaking because it was the best career position and salary she had ever achieved. Entering the job market at that time was difficult. Either there were no positions available in her field, or the jobs that were available offered only half of what she had been making before. We had to hold on and believe that God would make a way for her. The rest of 2008 and all of 2009 went by with no offers. It wasn't until August 2010 that a recruiter she had never heard of called to inform her of a position at an oil and gas company. Within a few days, she had an interview, and, a week later, she was hired as a temporary contractor, making almost the same salary as at her old job. All of this happened during the Sukkot offering.

During the last few months, the company has been so pleased with her work that she was being considered for a full-time position with the company. Prior to starting the job, she had been told that getting permanent positions with the company was difficult because resumes and permanent positions had to be approved by the board of directors.

We prayed that an offer would be extended by the end of 2010. Last week, she received an employment offer in writing: a major promotion and a raisc with a stock option. God has certainly provided our lives with His grace, financial favor, and favor with our fellow man. I can barely contain myself as I am writing this. We love the Lord with all of our hearts, and we praise Him for His goodness and for all that He has done in our lives.

Thirtyfold, Sixtyfold, and Hundredfold Blessings

There is one more concept related to how we go from thirtyfold to sixtyfold to hundredfold blessings. It is the Hebrew understanding that there is not one, not two, but three different ways in which we are to give. The first way is the tithe. According to Malachi 3:10, the Israelites were told to tithe *"that there may be food in My house."* The tithe was to fill the warehouse. The tithe was brought in so that the priests could present sacrifices for people who did not know God, as well as for those who could not afford to purchase their own sacrifices.

> **We tithe so that God's house can be full of people who do not yet know the sacrifice that was given for them through Jesus Christ.**

We tithe so that the church can afford to spread the gospel throughout the world. We tithe so that God's house can be full of people who do not yet know the sacrifice that was given for them through Jesus Christ. Your tithe is essential for the world to hear the gospel and receive the sacrifice of God.

The second way of giving is through the offerings that we bring three times each year, which were covered in this chapter.

But there is a third way.

Therefore do not worry, saying, "What shall we eat?" or "What shall we drink?" or "What shall we wear?" For after all these things the Gentiles seek. For your heavenly Father knows that you need all these things. But seek first the kingdom of God and His righteousness, and all these things shall be added to you.

(Matthew 6:31–33)

In Hebrew, the word *righteous* is translated as *tzedakah*, which means "acts of kindness." I'll expand on the *tzedakah* later, but, for now, let me say this: you'll never get a hundredfold blessing from God until you understand the tithe, the offering, and the acts of kindness. This is why Jesus didn't stop the poor widow from putting her last two mites into the offering.

And He looked up and saw the rich putting their gifts into the treasury, and He saw also a certain poor widow putting in two mites. So He said, "Truly I say to you that this poor widow has put in more than all; for all these out of their abundance have put in offerings for God, but she out of her poverty put in all the livelihood that she had." (Luke 21:1–4)

Jesus knew that this poor woman would never get into the flow of God's abundance until she first helped somebody else. He knew that her offering would release those blessings into her life.

Again, ancient Jewish wisdom tells us there are three things that have no limits. That's what the hundredfold blessing means: no limits! Let's review the three things that have no limits. One is the study of the Torah. You are doing that by reading this book. You are entering into a world of God's Word and revelation that has no limit. We haven't even touched the tip of the iceberg.

Number two is the giving of offerings, three times each year. God says, in effect, "Return to these offerings of old and watch Me open up the windows of heaven over your life and pour out a blessing until you have no room left, *'good measure, pressed down, shaken together, and running over'* (Luke 6:38). And not only that, I'll also rebuke the devourer to protect your entire household from his schemes."

Number three is acts of kindness, the "corner of the fields." Here, God says, "Don't hold on to all the harvest I give you. Help somebody else, for, when you do, your harvest will not be what you expect. Instead, it will be *'exceedingly abundantly above all that* [you] *ask or think'* (Ephesians 3:20). Enjoy the journey to your Promised Land. It really is *flowing* with milk, honey, and all good things!"

Testimonies of Firstfruits Offerings

Jeannie saw our television program and heard me talking about my last book, *The Torah Blessing*. Hearing about the Jewish roots of the Christian faith was new to Jeannie, but she said that it "grabbed hold of my heart and I had to get the book and read it." After reading the book, she began to experience a shift in her thinking about God and His plan for her life. She began to attend our church via the Internet, but, for our celebration of Sukkot, she drove over six hundred miles to attend our firstfruits service. During her visit, she gave an offering and purchased a *tallit*, or prayer shawl, with a new understanding of what God's Word teaches about meeting with Him at "appointed times." She said that following God's instructions about keeping the Sabbath and praying the tallit was like a dream. Within four months, her family's business was blessed financially to the point that they installed a beautiful in-ground swimming pool, and that's not all. It was completely paid for because of the additional business blessings they had received. Their business continued to increase, and, in August, they paid cash for a second home in Florida. Then, her husband paid off their car loan. She says that God has continued to prosper them in all areas of their life, not just their finances. Jeannie knows that God has a great plan for her family. She said that celebrating the Jewish roots of her faith has changed her family's life forever. And she knows that God's best is yet to come!

When we sow our firstfruits offerings to God and perform acts of kindness, the ceilings are removed from our lives. The limits are removed so that the God of blessings can pour abundance into our lives. When you bring your offerings, you divorce yourself from your old life of lack and limitation. No longer are you a slave, bound by the spirit of containment. Now, you have entered into a marriage relationship with God in which you become a partner, with all of the abundance of heaven.

A few years ago, one of our partners who watches our services on the Internet became extremely passionate about the Jewish roots of her faith. She began to celebrate the Sabbath in her home and eventually participated in our firstfruits offering. She obeyed God's instructions long before she fully understood what the Lord was trying to teach her through my ministry. Remember, God said to obey, and then the understanding would come. Even though these offerings occurred during the worldwide economic plunge, because of her obedience, she could see that her finances were not suffering. She was able to pay her bills on time and keep her office open in order to conduct business as an immigration assistant, citizenship instructor, and certified court interpreter. When she began to experience a dip in business, she asked the Lord for direction. Did He want her to close the office? She felt strongly that she was to stand firm. So, during Passover, she planted her firstfruits offering in the amount of one thousand dollars.

Afterward, the first thing she noticed was that a client who had left her business returned, asking for help. During the fifty days after Passover, God poured out a financial blessing into her life, far exceeding a thirtyfold, sixtyfold, or hundredfold increase. In fact, she told us that she experienced an increase of 110 percent! This allowed her to catch up on bills and to fly to Dallas to present her second firstfruits offering for our Pentecost service. She also gave us a list of other family members in different states who had been blessed by their obedience in the firstfruits offering.

A couple told us about the incredible story of a healing and a debt cancellation. One winter, the husband was diagnosed with pneumonia and hospitalized. His condition worsened, as none of the medications his doctor had prescribed seemed to work. Eventually, it became necessary to perform surgery to remove the bacteria and infection from his lungs. Although successful, the surgery left the couple with a hospital bill of around fifty thousand dollars. Since they were living off of a retirement pension, this bill was impossible for them to pay.

After he had recovered, the husband received a piece of mail from the hospital. What he expected to be another demand for payment of the debt turned out to be a letter informing him that one of the hospital's programs had paid the outstanding balance in full! This couple credits this absolute miracle of God to a teaching I had presented during the Sukkot season about God giving His people an extra thirty days to plant their firstfruits offering due to unforeseen circumstances. The unforeseen circumstance for this dear couple was a cash flow crunch. In the midst of their need, however, the wife had sowed a seed from what they called their "tiny retirement check," not knowing that her act of faith would open the windows of heaven and unleash a miraculous financial blessing. Now, this couple sees how God acted on their behalf to move a mountain of debt. Praise God, they were obedient because they knew that God is always faithful!

Part
III

Unveiling the
Ancient Mysteries

The *Tallit*:
Dwelling in the Secret Place

To enter into prayer is the most powerful way to relate to God. Think about it. Almighty God is inviting you and me to talk to Him about anything and everything.

I told the following story in my book *The Torah Blessing*, but I want to share it again with you. Tiz and I once stopped in Venice to do some research on our way back from Israel. While there, we visited Venice's original Jewish ghetto—the place where the word *ghetto* originated. I was waiting for Tiz outside a shop when these two young Jewish men approached and started talking to me. They asked about my prayer life and wanted to know if I had prayed that day. When I told them I had, they asked, "Have you prayed with *tefillin*?" This is the Hebrew practice of wrapping a strap of leather around your arm and another around your head when you pray. These men reminded me of Deuteronomy 6, where God instructed His people to pray this way.

> *Hear, O Israel: The LORD our God, the LORD is one! You shall love the LORD your God with all your heart, with all your soul, and with all your strength. And these words which I command you today shall be in your*

heart....You shall bind them as a sign on your hand,
and they shall be as frontlets between your eyes.

(Deuteronomy 6:4–6, 8)

I explained to the two men that I was the pastor of a church and had no knowledge of praying with the *tefillin*. I told them, "If you can tell me why you do this, not just out of ritual or legalism but from the true meaning of it, then I'll pray it with you." They smiled and said, "First, it slows us down and reminds us to think, *I'm about to talk to almighty God. He has invited me to talk with Him. He will stop all that He is doing, not only to listen to me, but also to speak back to me in my heart. Instead of being so busy, therefore, I need to slow down. God, my Father in heaven, wants to spend time with me.* Next, it reminds us that there are others who don't know God, who don't know that He loves them and wants to talk to them, too. I can't be satisfied that I, alone, talk to Him; I must also tell others."

Needless to say, we prayed together that day in Venice. It didn't matter to them that I was a Christian. We had a wonderful, loving discussion based on mutual respect and increased understanding.

Think about the power we have been given through prayer. Jewish wisdom teaches us that prayer, in its highest form and greatest sincerity, is called *avodah shebalev*, meaning "a service of the heart."

In Leviticus 20, God tells us, *"You shall be holy to Me, for I the LORD am holy, and have separated you from the peoples, that you should be Mine"* (verse 26). The word *holy* has two meanings in this verse. First, it is to be close to God. Second, it is to be separate from the world for God.

Now, let's unveil another one of God's secrets.

He who dwells in the secret place of the Most High
shall abide under the shadow of the Almighty. I will
say of the LORD, "He is my refuge and my fortress; my
God, in Him I will trust."   (Psalm 91:1–2)

For a long time, I thought that this Scripture was unfair. I thought, *God has a special place, but He is keeping it a secret?* The Hebrew word translated as *"secret place"* means "covering, shelter, hiding place, secrecy."

Now, look at what Jesus said in Matthew 6:6:

When you pray, go into your room, and when you have shut your door, pray to your Father who is in the secret place; and your Father who sees in secret will reward you openly.

Before we get to the tallit, let me repeat a teaching from my book *The Torah Blessing*.

Healing in His Wings

"Listen! Behold, a sower went out to sow. And it happened, as he sowed, that some seed fell by the wayside; and the birds of the air came and devoured it. Some fell on stony ground, where it did not have much earth; and immediately it sprang up because it had no depth of earth. But when the sun was up it was scorched, and because it had no root it withered away. And some seed fell among thorns; and the thorns grew up and choked it, and it yielded no crop. But other seed fell on good ground and yielded a crop that sprang up, increased and produced: some thirtyfold, some sixty, and some a hundred." And He said to them, "He who has ears to hear, let him hear!" (Mark 4:3–9)

This is the well-known parable of the seed and the sower. In it, Jesus was talking about seed falling on various types of soil. Then, all of a sudden, in verse 9, He declared, *"He who has ears to hear, let him hear!"* Obviously, Jesus was not addressing people who were actually missing physical ears. No, He was talking about people who heard the words He spoke but had no ability to understand. He was saying, in effect, "He who is anointed—touched and gifted by God with discernment and understanding—let him understand."

Can't you just see the apostles standing behind Him, nodding in agreement? Then, in the next verse, it says, *"When He was alone, those around Him with the twelve asked Him about the parable"* (Mark 4:10). His own disciples had no understanding. Jesus then said to them, *"To you it has been given to know the mystery of the kingdom of God; but to those who are outside, all things come in parables"* (verse 11). In other words, "To you who are born again, I am going to explain the mysteries of the kingdom of God, but to everyone else, these teachings are merely going to be stories."

Until we read and understand Scripture through Jesus' eyes—the eyes of *Yeshua*, the Messiah—and receive understanding by the Holy Spirit—the Spirit of the God of Abraham—the meaning of these teachings will remain locked in a neat little story. Let's ask God to help us go beyond the story to the place where the mystery of His Word is revealed.

"If Only I May Touch His Garment..."

The following story of healing is found in three of the four Gospels.

> *Now a certain woman had a flow of blood for twelve years, and had suffered many things from many physicians. She had spent all that she had and was no better, but rather grew worse.* (Mark 5:25–26)

Here was a woman who had suffered from a blood issue for twelve years. She had spent all of her money seeing every doctor and healer possible, but she could not get any better. She was about to try something that would prove she was at the end of her rope.

> *For she said to herself, "If only I may touch His garment, I shall be made well."* (Matthew 9:21)

Without going into graphic detail, let me just state that according to the Torah, a woman suffering from a flow of blood was considered to be "unclean." She was forbidden from appearing in public because anyone she touched was also viewed as unclean. Certainly, for such a woman to touch a rabbi was strictly forbidden. She had seen every doctor and had found no answer to her misery. Then, suddenly, she heard Jesus was coming. Imagine the desperation of this woman to enter a crowded public market full of witnesses in order to touch this visiting rabbi!

Perhaps you can relate to this woman. You don't feel worthy to go before a holy God, but you're desperate. You've tried everything, but you can't get your prosperity released, your debt cancelled, your kids serving God, or your husband to go to church. You can't find release from the bonds of sickness or addiction. You're sick and tired of being sick and tired. You've tried everything, and you're at the place where you are willing to try anything. You are desperate to find healing and wholeness.

The woman *"came from behind and touched the hem of His garment"* (Matthew 9:20). She thought, *If I can just touch the hem of His garment, my years of suffering and torment will be over.* The word for hem is *kraspedon*, meaning "a tassel of twisted wool." This woman wasn't even trying to touch the cloth of Jesus' garments, only the tassel of wool that hung off the side of His prayer shawl.

The Tallit

In the Old Testament, there is a brief command: *"You shall make tassels on the four corners of the clothing with which you cover yourself"* (Deuteronomy 22:12). This is a strange little commandment in the middle of the chapter instructing the men of Israel in what to wear. No more explanation is given. It is preceded and followed by other aspects of Mosaic law. In Numbers, however, the command is expanded:

Again the LORD spoke to Moses, saying, "Speak to the children of Israel: Tell them to make tassels on the corners of their garments throughout their generations, and to put a blue thread in the tassels of the corners. And you shall have the tassel, that you may look upon it and remember all the commandments of the LORD and do them." (Numbers 15:37–39)

Therefore, *"throughout their generations,"* Jewish men were instantly recognizable by the tassels of twisted wool on the fringes of their outer garments. Jesus was no different.

Switching now to Luke's account of the story, the woman *"came from behind and touched the border of His garment. And immediately her flow of blood stopped"* (Luke 8:44).

The traditional Jewish shawl with tassels on the four corners is called the *tallit*. The woven tassels represent the 613 commandments, or mitzvahs, of God, which protect, lead, guide, and teach His people. Jesus, as a Jewish man who was called "Rabbi," certainly would have worn such a shawl. The English translation of the edge of the tallit is *"border,"* but in Hebrew, it is also referred to as the *arba kanfot*, or "four wings."

Imagine this woman, who had grown up hearing stories of a coming Messiah. She had heard men speaking of the prophecies in Isaiah about one who was *"wounded for our transgressions,...bruised for our iniquities; the chastisement for our peace was upon Him, and by His stripes we are healed"* (Isaiah 53:5). When she saw Jesus wearing the prayer shawl, she knew, based on God's promises, that she would finally receive the miracle she had been seeking for so long. She had heard the prophecy that said, *"The Sun of Righteousness shall arise with healing in His wings"* (Malachi 4:2). She didn't try to brush his sleeve. She didn't cry out from afar. She knew the prophecy and had faith that God would be true to His Word, so she reached out and grabbed it. I'm sure it wasn't much of a touch. She'd suffered from bleeding for *twelve years*! She was probably sickly, thin, and weak in her appearance. Yet she reached out and grabbed that promise of God as it passed by her. And Jesus immediately stopped.

> Jesus said, "Who touched Me?" When all denied it, Peter and those with him said, "Master, the multitudes throng and press You, and You say, 'Who touched Me?'" But Jesus said, "Somebody touched Me, for I perceived power going out from Me." (Luke 8:45–46)

When the woman touched the hem of His tallit, Jesus *felt* the power go out. I don't know about you, but I would like to get in on some of that power!

> Now when the woman saw that she was not hidden, she came trembling; and falling down before Him, she declared to Him in the presence of all the people the reason she had touched Him and how she was healed immediately. And He said to her, "Daughter, be of good cheer; your faith has made you well. Go in peace."
>
> (verses 47–48)

Jesus didn't know this woman. He had never met her. Yet she knew that the Messiah would come—that Jesus would come—with healing in His wings.

Is it preposterous to believe that when we obey God's Word and wear a reminder of His promises when we pray, He will bring healing in the wings of the tallit? You might think, *Why would we need something so external in order to facilitate God's healing?*

Is it true that when we anoint people with oil, they will be healed? (See, for example, James 5:14.)

Is it true that when we lay hands on the sick, they will recover? (See, for example, Mark 16:18.)

Is it true that we should put guards on our mouths, for there is life and death in the power of the tongue? (See Proverbs 18:21.)

Is there any use in rejoicing in the Lord always, for God inhabits the praises of His people? (See Philippians 4:4; Psalm 22:3 KJV.)

Is it true that our tithes and offerings will open up the windows of heaven? (See Malachi 3:10.)

Is it true that when we sing praises to God, He is there in our midst?

Does God manifest His presence and power in all of these outward expressions? Yes?

Then, perhaps God has given us another revelation. You don't have to do any of those things for your salvation. You don't have to anoint with oil or lay hands on the sick or tithe or sing praises to God. However, the Bible says,

> *Be doers of the word, and not hearers only, deceiving yourselves....But he who...continues in it, and is not a forgetful hearer but a doer of the work, this one will be blessed in what he does.* (James 1:22, 25)

The Secret Place

Let me share with you a tremendous revelation that has changed my life and will change yours, too. Here, in two Scriptures, we read about a "secret place." In Matthew, Jesus was speaking to Jewish people who already understood what the secret place was and where it could be found. This is just another perfect illustration of the fact that we cannot fully understand the New Testament until we understand the Old Testament. We also can't fully understand what Jesus taught until we fully understand what Moses taught.

> *He who dwells in the secret place of the Most High shall abide under the shadow of the Almighty....He shall cover you with His feathers, and under His wings you shall take refuge; His truth shall be your shield and buckler.* (Psalm 91:1, 4)

Earlier, we read about the woman with the issue of blood being healed as she touched the hem of Jesus' garment—His tallit. Now, we are reading about taking refuge under His feathers and wings.

When we wear the tallit, we dwell in the secret place of the Most High God. In His shadow—under His wings—we find refuge, healing, deliverance, and prosperity. It has always been a tradition to pray under the tallit, "How precious is Your kindness, O God. Mankind is in the shelter of Your wings." Of course, we know that

> **When we wear the tallit, we dwell in the secret place of the Most High God.**

God is not a bird with feathers, but this is not just an analogy—it is prophetic.

God wants us to be holy, separated from the world for Him, especially when we pray. Wearing a tallit is a very powerful way to do that. When you cover your head with a tallit, you are entering into a "secret place." As you cover your face, you *"shut your door"*:

> *When you pray, go into your room, and when you have* **shut your door***, pray to your Father who is in the* **secret place***; and your Father who sees in secret will reward you openly.*   (Matthew 6:6, emphasis added)

Ancient Jewish wisdom says that when you *"shut your door,"* you are separated from the distractions and influence of the world. The enemy is not allowed to speak to your mind or bring about doubt and confusion while you pray. Why is this so important? Remember what James said:

> *If any of you lacks wisdom, let him ask of God, who gives to all liberally and without reproach, and it will be given to him. But let him ask in faith, with no doubting, for he who doubts is like a wave of the sea driven and tossed by the wind. For let not that man suppose*

that he will receive anything from the Lord; he is a double-minded man, unstable in all his ways.

(James 1:5–8)

When you enter into *"the secret place"* and *"shut your door,"* God covers you with protection so that you won't be double-minded. Then, in this isolation with God, you start receiving the answers you have been seeking.

Don't get me wrong; you can pray to God anytime, anyplace, and He will hear you and bless you. But in these last days, our eyes are being opened and God is showing us something new and fresh. He is drawing us back to His *"secret place."*

I can remember a time when Tiz and I were appearing on a television show and the host asked us about my teaching called "Healing in His Wings." I told him about the secret place of God. When I got to what Jesus said in Matthew 6, the man's eyes lit up. He said, "I get it now! I've been to Israel many times and have often wondered what Jesus was saying. How could they go into their closets to pray? They didn't have closets in those days. The closet—the secret place—was the *tallit*, the same garment Jesus wore when the woman with the issue of blood touched the hem of His garment and received healing!" (See Mark 5:25–34; Luke 8:43–48.)

Let me say it again: you don't have to wear a tallit to pray to God. But let me also ask, what if there were a way to "supercharge" your prayers? I'm reminded of a friend of mine who is around seventy years old and has been a strong Christian for many years. Recently, he said to me, "Larry, I bought a tallit and prayed under it for the first time. To be honest with you, I didn't think it would make any difference at all. I didn't think that such things were for Christians anymore. But God kept speaking to me and asking me to do it. So, I did. Never before have I felt God in my life more than when I prayed under the tallit. My half-hour prayer turned into three hours. It was amazing!"

Let me encourage you to give it a try. You may contact our ministry to order a tallit. Go into *"the secret place," "shut your door"* so you won't be *"double-minded,"* and see if God's Word is true when Jesus says, *"And your Father who sees in secret will reward you openly"* (Matthew 6:6).

God wants to bless us by revealing not only the secrets to physical healing in His wings but also the secrets to all kinds of other blessings, including financial blessings and outpourings of His resources and abundance. Where is this end-time wealth coming from? Let me give you a hint: *"I will give you the treasures of darkness and hidden riches of secret places, that you may know that I, the LORD, who call you by name, am the God of Israel"* (Isaiah 45:3). When you find the secret place, God will show you where your treasure and riches have been hidden until now! When you come into that secret place to pray to God and hear from Him, He will give you *"knowledge of witty inventions"* (Proverbs 8:12 KJV). He will reveal to you ideas, concepts, and insights that will influence others and bless your life!

> *For in the time of trouble He shall hide me in His pavilion; in the secret place of His tabernacle He shall hide me; He shall set me high upon a rock.* (Psalm 27:5)

The woman with the issue of blood was healed when she touched Jesus' tallit. Let me point out that this was not just a one-time occurrence. There are many accounts in the New Testament of people receiving healing while praying under the tallit. (See, for example, Matthew 14:36; Mark 6:56.) By this, we can see that praying under the tallit to release God's power was not just intended for biblical times but all times. These healings were not meant to be a one-time occurrence but an everyday occurrence, even now, every day of our lives. Let me share a few testimonies of people in our ministry who are living proof of God's healing power!

If Jesus felt it was necessary to pray under the tallit and saw these kinds of results, shouldn't we, too, pray this way? Here in Dallas, we call this a clue! God has made this tremendous power available to you and me and has set up specific ways for us to access it. For every need we face, the Lord has an answer. For every challenge we face, He has a miracle. Let's tap into all that the Lord has intended for our lives, our families, our health, and our finances. Let's enter into that secret place and discover the fullness of God's blessings!

The *Mezuzah*:
Your World and a Higher Force

Many people think being spiritual consists in giving away all that you own and living in some monastery in the mountains. But God says, "Keep your home, your marriage, your kids, and your career, and take them all to a higher level." In Hebrew, this is called a *mitzvah*, or a commandment. It is something that God tells us to do. A *mitzvah* is a connection between your world and a higher power.

> *Beloved, I pray that you may prosper in all things and be in health, just as your soul prospers.* (3 John 1:2)

God's goal is for you to get everything good out of life. He wants you to prosper and be in health. But the key is that your soul prospers as you dive deeper into the knowledge of God's Word. If you are willing to learn, you can go even deeper into the revelation of God's Word.

Ancient Jewish wisdom suggests that the idea of looking for a deeper meaning in the Torah—the Bible—is no different from looking for a deeper meaning in the sciences. Just as we look for deeper meanings and truths in the workings of nature, we also need to look for deeper truths as we read the Bible. King Solomon alluded to this in Proverbs 25:11: *"A word fitly spoken is like apples of gold in settings of silver."* In his book *The Guide for the Perplexed*, Moses Maimonides explains this proverb. According to Maimonides, the setting of silver represents the text of the Torah, as seen from a distance. The apples of gold are the secrets held within the Torah text.

Thousands of years ago, the author of Hebrews discerned a difference between the *"milk"* and the *"meat"* of learning about the things of God.

> *For everyone who partakes only of milk is unskilled in the word of righteousness, for he is a babe. But solid food ["strong meat" KJV] belongs to those who are of full age, that is, those who by reason of use have their senses exercised to discern both good and evil.*
>
> (Hebrews 5:13–14)

Let me show you one of the greatest secrets that God is unveiling for us in these last days.

> *Now this is the commandment, and these are the statutes and judgments which the LORD your God has commanded to teach you, that you may observe them in the land which you are crossing over to possess, that you may fear the LORD your God, to keep all His statutes and His commandments which I command you, you and your son and your grandson, all the days of your life, and that your days may be prolonged. Therefore hear, O Israel, and be careful to observe it, that it may be well with you, and that you may multiply greatly as the LORD God of your fathers has promised you; "a land flowing with milk and honey." Hear, O Israel: The LORD our God, the LORD is one! You shall love the LORD your God with all your heart, with all your soul, and with all your strength. And these words which I command you today shall be in your heart. You shall teach them diligently to your children, and shall talk of them when you sit in your house, when you walk by the way, when you lie down, and when you rise*

up. You shall bind them as a sign on your hand, and they shall be as frontlets between your eyes. You shall write them on the doorposts of your house and on your gates. (Deuteronomy 6:1–9)

In Hebrew, the word for Scripture that appears on the doorpost of a building is *mezuzah*, which literally means "doorpost." If you have ever been to Israel or to a Jewish neighborhood, home, or restaurant, you have probably seen a *mezuzah* on the upper right side of every door. A *mezuzah* is not a "lucky charm" but a powerful reminder that God tells us to take His Word and put it on the doorposts of our homes.

Inevitably, whenever I teach this, someone asks, "Pastor Larry, is this for us? Does it really make any difference if I take some of God's Word and attach it to the doorpost of my house?" I always answer this question with a question.

Suppose someone gives you a book on witchcraft that teaches how to put curses on other people. Would you allow this book in your home? You don't have to read it; you don't ever have to open it. It would just sit on your coffee table or your kitchen counter or your child's bookshelf. Would you leave it there? I'm pretty sure that most would answer, "No. There's no way I would allow a book like that in my home!" Isn't it "just a book"? You don't believe in it and probably wouldn't read it. So, what would be the harm?

Most people would probably say, "That book would bring a bad spirit into my house." And they would be right!

Now, let's look at the other side of that argument. If evil words carry a bad spirit with them, then good words have a good spirit connected to them. I sometimes preach a message entitled "Please, Take Out the Garbage." In it, I urge people to go through their homes and cleanse them of every book, souvenir, gift, and anything else that might have an evil spirit attached to it. Most Christians are aware of the importance of keeping bad spirits away from their homes and families. Here, God tells us how to release His Spirit into every room of our homes, which is just as important, if not more so. (See, for example, Matthew 12:43–45.)

On each Hebrew mezuzah is written all or part of one of the following Scripture passages:

Hear, O Israel: The LORD our God, the LORD is one! You shall love the LORD your God with all your heart, with all your soul, and with all your strength. And these words which I command you today shall be in your heart. You shall teach them diligently to your children, and shall talk of them when you sit in your house, when you walk by the way, when you lie down, and when you rise up. You shall bind them as a sign on your hand, and they shall be as frontlets between your eyes. You shall write them on the doorposts of your house and on your gates.   (Deuteronomy 6:4–9)

And it shall be that if you earnestly obey My commandments which I command you today, to love the LORD your God and serve Him with all your heart and with all your soul, then I will give you the rain for your land in its season, the early rain and the latter rain, that you may gather in your grain, your new wine, and your oil. And I will send grass in your fields for your livestock, that you may eat and be filled. Take heed to yourselves, lest your heart be deceived, and you turn aside and serve other gods and worship them, lest the Lord's anger be aroused against you, and He shut up the heavens so that there be no rain, and the land yield no produce, and you perish quickly from the good land which the LORD is giving you. Therefore you shall lay up these words of mine in your heart and in your soul, and bind them as a sign on your hand, and they shall be as frontlets between your eyes. You shall teach them to your children, speaking of them when you sit in your house, when you walk by the way, when you lie down, and when you rise up. And you shall write them on the doorposts of your house and on your gates, that your days and the days of your children may be multiplied in the land of which the LORD swore to your fathers to give them, like the days of the heavens above the earth.

(Deuteronomy 11:13–21)

Notice what God told His people to put on the doorposts of their homes: God is our God, He loves us, and we need to look to Him always. We need to teach our children about God and His goodness. He will bring us prosperity, protection, provision, health, victory, and long life. Every time you walk through the door of your home, God's words are there to bless you in your coming and in your going.

> **Every time you walk through the door of your home, God's words are there to bless you in your coming and in your going.**

Years ago, when my daughter Katie was about ten or eleven, she had a friend staying overnight in our house. As they were walking into Katie's room, I heard her friend ask about the "little box" that was on the frame of her door. I was interested in hearing what Katie would say about it. She said, "Oh, that's a mezuzah." The friend asked, "What's it for?" Katie replied, "It's to remind me that no matter what I am going through, God is there to bless me in my coming and in my going." I was so proud of her. Even at that young age, Katie understood what it meant to have God's Word on the doorpost of her room. It was what she said next, however, that made me even prouder. She said, "It also reminds me that in order to be blessed, I need to be a blessing to others as I go into the world, and then, I need to be a blessing when I come back to my house."

The Supernatural

Let me say again, a mezuzah is not a "lucky charm." God does, however, honor our obedience to His Word, just as He does when we…

- Lay hands on the sick
- Honor Him in our hearts with praise and worship
- Anoint people with oil
- Guard the words of our mouths

Again, is there an anointing of supernatural healing when we put our hands on someone and pray for a miracle? Of course there is. Can our circumstances change if we lift up our hands and praise God? Absolutely. Can God work a miracle when we anoint someone with oil? Sure, He can. Can we release life or death just by the words we speak? You bet. (See Proverbs 18:21.) How do we know these things are real? Because God said so in His Word.

> *"For My thoughts are not your thoughts, nor are your ways My ways," says the LORD. "For as the heavens are higher than the earth, so are My ways higher than your ways, and My thoughts than your thoughts."*
>
> (Isaiah 55:8–9)

If God says, "Trust Me. Go ahead and lay hands on the sick, praise Me in hard times, anoint others with oil, and guard the words you speak," can't we also trust the same God when He tells us to take His Word and put it on the doorposts of our homes?

As I convey these truths, I try not to just unveil the secrets I have found but also to answer some of the same questions I had when I first started to discover these biblical teachings. For instance, since this was taught to the Jewish people of the Old Testament, is it still for us today? I say that not only this teaching but all of God's teachings are still for us today. This is true for each "new" secret in this book. We are now a part of the family of Israel.

> *But they have not all obeyed the gospel. For Isaiah says, "Lord, who has believed our report?" So then faith comes by hearing, and hearing by the word of*

God. But I say, have they not heard? Yes indeed: "Their sound has gone out to all the earth, and their words to the ends of the world." (Romans 10:16–18)

Till all come to the unity of the faith and of the knowledge of the Son of God, to a perfect man, to the measure of the stature of the fullness of Christ.

(Ephesians 4:13)

Grafted into Them

Remember, as a Christian, you have been grafted into Israel. You are an heir of the promises of Abraham. So, when we talk about Israel and Jewish ways, even if you're a Christian, your faith comes from a Jewish heritage. It doesn't matter if you're white, brown, or black. It doesn't matter what denomination you are. You are grafted into Israel and heirs of the promises made to Abraham.

> **It doesn't matter if you're white, brown, or black. It doesn't matter what denomination you are. You are grafted into Israel and heirs of the promises made to Abraham.**

For if the firstfruit is holy, the lump is also holy; and if the root is holy, so are the branches. And if some of the branches were broken off, and you, being a wild olive tree, were grafted in among them, and with them became a partaker of the root and fatness of the olive tree, do not boast against the branches. But if you do boast, remember that you do not support the root, but the root supports you. You will say then, "Branches were broken off that I might be grafted in." Well said. Because of unbelief they were broken off, and you stand by faith. Do not be haughty, but fear. For if God did not spare the natural branches, He may not spare you either. (Romans 11:16–21)

In an excellent teaching on the mezuzah in his book *Understanding Judaism: A Basic Guide to Jewish Faith, History, and Practice*, Rabbi Mordechai Katz says it is obligatory for Jewish men and women (and now, you, too, because you have been grafted in) to have a mezuzah on their doors at all times. The mezuzah officially dedicates our dwellings to the Almighty. Just as all aspects of our lives must be sanctified, so must our homes be sanctified. Like the flag on an embassy, the mezuzah represents God's presence in a particular place in the world.

There is supernatural happiness that awaits you when God opens your eyes and unveils the secrets of His kingdom in the last days. In Proverbs 3, it says, *"Happy is the man who finds wisdom, and the man who gains understanding"* (verse 13). Happy is the man or woman who finds wisdom and gains understanding. Have you ever asked, "What am I missing?" God showed me that I needed to *"Get wisdom! Get understanding!"* (Proverbs 4:5).

> And they shall take some of the blood and put it on the two doorposts and on the lintel of the houses where they eat it....For the LORD will pass through to strike the Egyptians; and when He sees the blood on the lintel and on the two doorposts, the LORD will pass over the door and not allow the destroyer to come into your houses to strike you.   (Exodus 12:7, 23)

At Passover, God told His people that when He saw the blood on the doorposts of their homes, He would pass over and not destroy them. In the *Mechilta*, a commentary on the book of Exodus written in the third century, it says, "Now consider: The blood of the Passover sacrifice was but of little weight, for it was required but once, not for all generations, and by night only, not by day; yet He would *'not allow the destroyer...to strike you.'* How much more will He not permit the destroyer into the house which bears a mezuzah, which is of greater weight, seeing that the Divine Name is repeated there ten times, it is there by day and night, and it is a law for all generations."

If we add to our faith in the blood of Jesus this hidden knowledge of obeying God by writing His name ten times on the doorposts of our homes, we will experience supernatural protection. Immediately after God told His children to place His Word on the doorposts of their homes, He promised *"that your days and the days of your children may be multiplied in the land of which the* LORD *swore to your fathers to give them, like the days of the heavens above the earth"* (Deuteronomy 11:21).

Something supernatural happens when we obey God. We don't understand it; we just know that if God tells us to do it, and we obey, He will always back up His Word. It's the same way with the mezuzah. I don't understand how it works; I just know that it does.

> *What man is there who has built a new house and has not dedicated it* [with a mezuzah]? *Let him go and return to his house, lest he die in the battle and another man dedicate it.* (Deuteronomy 20:5)

You are in a battle. It is a battle for your family, your children, your finances, and your health. When you put God's Word on the doorposts of your home, God says, "The enemy will not be permitted in to smite you. You will be blessed in your coming and in your going." Even though we have Jesus in our hearts, we still need to tithe our 10 percent, we still need to put a guard on our mouths, we still need to rejoice in the Lord always, and we still need to put God's Word on the doorposts of our homes. We don't have to do any of these things unless we want to win the battle.

> *For we do not wrestle against flesh and blood, but against principalities, against powers, against the rulers of the darkness of this age, against spiritual hosts of wickedness in the heavenly places.* (Ephesians 6:12)

Because of that, the weapons we use are not carnal but mighty.

*For the weapons of our warfare are not carnal but
mighty in God for pulling down strongholds.*

(2 Corinthians 10:4)

When you affix the mezuzah to your doorpost, it is to be in
the upper right. Why? *"The Lord is your keeper; the Lord is your
shade at your right hand"* (Psalm 121:5).

The Talmud relates the following story. The last Parthian
King, Ardavan IV, sent a pearl of purest radiance to a rabbi
named Yehudah HaNasi. With it, the king requested that the
rabbi send him something equally precious in return. HaNasi
sent him a mezuzah. Ardavan sent back word: "I sent you
something beyond price, and you sent me something that sells
for a debased coin of no value!" HaNasi replied, "My desirable
things and thy desirable things are not to be compared. You
sent me something that I must guard, whereas I sent you something that guards you as you sleep. As it is said: *'When you
roam, they will lead you; when you sleep, they will keep you'*
(Proverbs 6:22)."

Rabbeinu Bachya writes,

To impart in our hearts the principle that Divine protection pervades Israel at all times, day and night, the
Torah has commanded us to place the mezuzah at the
entrance of our homes. We will thus be cognizant of
this principle of Divine protection whenever we enter
a home, and we will be mindful that this protection
is constantly with us. Even at night, His protection
surrounds our house and protects us while we sleep.[4]

Ancient Jewish wisdom tells us that God is supreme above
all and rules over the six ends of the universe: above, beneath,
north, south, east, and west. Likewise, the psalmist mentions
the six ways in which God protects us:

---

[4]Alexander Poltorak, "The Protective Power of Mezuzah," www.chabad.org/library/article_cdo/
aid/310889.

Behold, He who keeps Israel shall neither slumber nor sleep. The LORD is your keeper; the LORD is your shade at your right hand. The sun shall not strike you by day, nor the moon by night. The LORD shall preserve you from all evil; He shall preserve your soul. The LORD shall preserve your going out and your coming in from this time forth, and even forevermore. (Psalm 121:4–8)

Concerning your home or business, God says,

This is the gate of the LORD, through which the righteous shall enter. (Psalm 118:20)

Another famous rabbi wrote that unlike the commandments, such as honoring one's parents, for which the promised reward is longevity, the act of affixing a mezuzah does not reap a future reward but an immediate reward of protection.

> **The act of affixing a mezuzah does not reap a future reward but an immediate reward of protection.**

By this point, you are probably thinking, *Larry, do you really believe something supernatural will happen when we put a mezuzah, God's Word, on the doorposts of our homes?* Absolutely, I do! Just as I believe God will honor His Word when, by faith, we pay our tithes, lay hands on the sick, and place a guard on our mouths. Nothing ever happens out of religious ritual but through revelation. God said, *"Be doers of the word, and not hearers only"* (James 1:22). If God says, *"Rejoice in the Lord always"* (Philippians 4:4), we should do it. If He tells us to bring an offering three times each year so that He can open the windows of heaven over our lives, I say, "Let's do it!" Likewise, if God says to write His Word *"on the doorposts of your house"* (Deuteronomy 11:20), again, I say, "Let's do it!" Let's take God at His word when He promises to *"preserve your going out and your coming in from this time forth, and even forevermore"* (Psalm 121:8). Let's take Him at His word when He promises to bring us prosperity and health and to protect our children from the enemy. Let's do it. Let's start walking every day in the protection and promises of God!

> *Then the* Lord *said to me, "You have seen well, for I am ready to perform My word."* (Jeremiah 1:12)

God is not only faithful to His Word, but He is also *"ready to perform"* it! I once told Bible scholar Rabbi David Lapin about another rabbi I had met. This other rabbi had told me, "I went to your Web site. Why are you teaching about Shabbat, tallit, and mezuzahs?" I love how Rabbi Lapin responded. He said, "Next time a rabbi asks you why you are teaching about these things, ask him, 'Why aren't you?'"

My prayer is that your eyes will be opened, that you will be one of the "children of miracles," and that, through the blessing of God's power in your life, you will draw multitudes back to Him.

Modeh Ani:
The Rudder of Your Day

The first ten minutes of your morning can change the course of your entire day.

It's no secret that, as the children of God, we ought to pray every day. Even better, we ought to start every day with prayer.

> *If My people who are called by My name will humble themselves, and pray and seek My face, and turn from their wicked ways, then I will hear from heaven, and will forgive their sin and heal their land.*
>
> (2 Chronicles 7:14)

As Christians, we know that God calls us to slow down, stop what we are doing, and take time to talk with Him. And yet, too often, we don't seem to be able to find the time in our hectic schedules for quality fellowship with the Lord.

> *Then* [Jesus] *came to the disciples and found them asleep, and said to Peter, "What? Could you not watch with Me one hour?"* (Matthew 26:40)

Most of us are dads and moms; husbands and wives; people with jobs, businesses, and families to run. How do we shoulder all of the responsibilities of these roles and still find the time to pray?

We have read Scriptures like Matthew 26:40 and been motivated to say, "You're right, Lord. I'm going to set aside one hour every morning to pray to You." And, although we mean it at the time, reality sets in and the alarm goes off. Then, we race around to get ready for work. We have to get the kids up, dressed, and fed; make sure their teeth are brushed and their hair is combed; and send them off to school on time. Later in the day, there are car pools, practices, rehearsals, supper, homework, bathing, and bedtime. Before you know it, the day is gone and you're exhausted.

Most of us would gladly pray an hour every day if God would give us twenty-seven hours in a day instead of only twenty-four. As a pastor, I'm blessed to have a job that requires me to pray and spend time in God's Word. Even so, every pastor knows the feeling of getting so busy *working* for God that it's hard to find the time for *talking* with God.

Not long ago, as I was preparing to teach on the Hebrew revelation of prayer, I read an article called "Rudder of the Day" by Yaakov Lieder.[5] It referenced a study that concluded that the first few minutes after we wake up are the "rudder" of our day. These minutes determine the outlook and direction of the rest of our day. It wasn't talking about when we've been awake for a while and have showered, dressed, and eaten breakfast. It said that the initial thoughts that pass through our minds as soon as we wake up determine our thinking and actions for the rest of the day. They determine whether we will have a positive or a negative day, a productive day or a wasteful day.

> *Eat thou not the bread of him that hath an evil eye, neither desire thou his dainty meats: for as he thinketh in his heart, so is he: Eat and drink, saith he to thee; but his heart is not with thee.*

> (Proverbs 23:6–7 ᴋᴊᴠ)

More modern translations say, *"Do not eat the bread of a miser"* (ɴᴋᴊᴠ), but I like the translation *"Eat thou not the bread*

[5]www.chabad.org/library/article_cdo/aid/36277.

of him that hath an evil eye" better. Don't eat with people who see all the negative things of the world. What you think about in your heart will be reproduced in your day. According to this study, what you focus on as you first wake up sets your course, like a rudder that guides a ship during a storm and gets it safely to the dock so that it doesn't crash into the rocks. So, it is important that you don't rush to turn on the news as soon as you awake. These days, the reports you find on television, the radio, and the Internet are seldom good news.

When I was a teenager, a friend of mine fell off a cliff that we had been climbing. The fall severely injured his leg. Two of us who were there put our Boy Scout training to use and stopped the bleeding so that we could carry him out of the woods and get him to a hospital. His doctors said that what we had done in those first few minutes not only saved his leg but also saved his life. His father asked the local newspaper to run a story on how some teenage boys saved a life—some good news about teenagers, for a change. I'll never forget what that man from the newspaper told him: "Good news doesn't sell."

> **What you focus on as you first wake up sets your course, like a rudder that guides a ship during a storm and gets it safely to the dock so that it doesn't crash into the rocks.**

If you turn on the news first thing in the morning, what you're likely to hear are stories about wars, earthquakes, accidents, murders, political scandals, business concerns about crashes and interest rates, or the plummeting value of your homes. If there isn't enough negative local news to report, you can be sure the news teams will travel far and wide to dig up enough bad news to get your day started in a negative way.

According to Yaakov Lieder's article, the researchers' advice was to "wake up to some soft music, say a prayer and read some positive literature, thereby filling up the first ten minutes of your day with positive thoughts."[6]

---

[6]Ibid.

Of course, there's even a better way to get your spiritual rudder in the water.

Modeh Ani

Ancient Jewish wisdom calls it *modeh ani*. It means "I acknowledge," or "I give thanks." And it will change your day and your life. Here's how it works:

The moment you awake, say a prayer like this:

I offer thanks to You, living and eternal King, for You have restored my soul within me; Your faithfulness is great!

Or, phonetically, in Hebrew:

Modeh anee lifanecha melech chai vikayam, she-he-chezarta bee nishmatee b'cherila, raba emunatecha.

Before my foot hits the floor in the morning, my first thoughts and words give praise to God. You might ask, "Larry, what am I praising God for?" Well, first, for life—you are alive, praise God! But you are also praising Him for all the plans He has for you that day. Ancient Jewish wisdom teaches that while we are sleeping, God is refreshing our souls and our spirits.

I will both lie down in peace, and sleep; for You alone,
O LORD, make me dwell in safety. (Psalm 4:8)

I've learned to start my daily journey spiritually by making my first words and thoughts those of praise: "modeh ani." There are times when I awake and start to get out of bed, but then, I stop, get back under the covers, and begin to praise God. I praise Him for life and for the great plans He has for me. I praise Him for my wife, Tiz, for my kids, and for the "sugars," my grandchildren. I praise Him for His goodness and blessings. Before I put one foot on the ground, I'm already entering into the blessings and miracles He has for me through praise and thanksgiving.

Enter into His gates with thanksgiving, and into His courts with praise. Be thankful to Him, and bless His name. (Psalm 100:4)

Start your day with good news, not bad news!

After I've taken a few minutes to praise the Lord and thank Him for His plans for me today, I am ready to get out of bed and start my morning. I still refrain from turning on the television or the radio, however. Most mornings, I'm the first one up in my household, but even if I'm not, I find a place where I can be by myself. Before I begin my personal prayers, I read the Scriptures that ancient Jewish wisdom tells us to start our days by reading.

Hear, O Israel: the LORD our God, the LORD is one! You shall love the LORD your God with all your heart, with all your soul, and with all your strength. And these words which I command you today shall be in your heart. You shall teach them diligently to your children, and shall talk of them when you sit in your house, when you walk by the way, when you lie down, and when you rise up. You shall bind them as a sign on your hand, and they shall be as frontlets between your eyes. You shall write them on the doorposts of your house and on your gates. (Deuteronomy 6:4–9)

And it shall be that if you earnestly obey My commandments which I command you today, to love the LORD your God and serve Him with all your heart and with all your soul, then I will give you the rain for your land in its season, the early rain and the latter rain, that you may gather in your grain, your new wine, and your oil. And I will send grass in your fields for your livestock, that you may eat and be filled. Take heed to yourselves, lest your heart be deceived, and you turn aside and serve other gods and worship them, lest the Lord's anger be aroused against you, and He shut up the heavens so that there be no rain, and the land yield no produce, and you perish quickly from the good land which the LORD is giving you. Therefore you shall lay up these words of mine in your heart and in your soul, and bind them as a sign on your hand, and they shall be as frontlets between your eyes. You shall teach them to your children, speaking of them when you sit in your house, when you walk by the way, when you lie down, and when you rise up. And you shall write them on the doorposts of your house and on your gates, that your days and the days of your children may be multiplied in the land of which the LORD swore to your fathers to give them, like the days of the heavens above the earth.

(Deuteronomy 11:13–21)

Again the LORD spoke to Moses, saying, "Speak to the children of Israel: Tell them to make tassels on the corners of their garments throughout their generations, and to put a blue thread in the tassels of the corners. And you shall have the tassel, that you may look upon it and remember all the commandments of the LORD and do them, and that you may not follow the harlotry to which your own heart and your own eyes are inclined, and that you may remember and do all My commandments, and be holy for your God. I am the LORD your God, who brought you out of the land of Egypt, to be your God: I am the LORD your God."

(Numbers 15:37–41)

These are some of the Scriptures that we are taught to read first thing in the morning. Not only are we to read them, but we are also to pray them. They are the Word of God, and prayer causes them to come alive for us. Personally, I like to read a longer excerpt from Deuteronomy 6.

Now this is the commandment, and these are the statutes and judgments which the LORD your God has commanded to teach you, that you may observe them in the land which you are crossing over to possess, that you may fear the LORD your God, to keep all His statutes and His commandments which I command you, you and your son and your grandson, all the days of your life, and that your days may be prolonged. Therefore hear, O Israel, and be careful to observe it, that it may be well with you, and that you may multiply greatly as the LORD God of your fathers has promised you; "a land flowing with milk and honey." Hear, O Israel: The LORD our God, the LORD is one! You shall love the LORD your God with all your heart, with all your soul, and with all your strength. And these words which I command you today shall be in your heart. You shall teach them diligently to your children, and shall talk of them when you sit in your house, when you walk by the way, when you lie down, and when you rise up. You shall bind them as a sign on your hand, and they shall be as frontlets between your eyes. You shall write them on the doorposts of your house and on your gates. So it shall be, when the LORD your God brings you into the land of which He swore to your fathers, to Abraham, Isaac, and Jacob, to give you large and beautiful cities which you did not build, houses full of all good things, which you did not fill, hewn-out wells which you did not dig, vineyards and olive trees which you did not plant; when you have eaten and are full; then beware, lest you forget the LORD who brought you out of the land of Egypt, from the house of bondage.

(Deuteronomy 6:1–12)

Next to God, the most important thing in my life is my family. In verse 2 of this passage, I proclaim that my children, my grandchildren, and I will serve God all our lives. Instead of starting my day by hearing about divorce, adultery, abuse, and other problems, I fill my thoughts with the Word of God, which says that my extended family will serve Him. Moses said, *"You* shall love the LORD your God with all your heart, with all your soul, and with all your strength. And these words which I command you today shall be in your heart. You shall teach them diligently to your children, and shall talk of them when you sit in your house, when you walk by the way, when you lie down, and when you rise up" (Deuteronomy 6:5–7). Then, when you wake your kids for school, they will rise with a spirit of peace and blessing.

> Then I will give you the rain for your land in its season, the early rain and the latter rain, that you may gather in your grain, your new wine, and your oil.
>
> (Deuteronomy 11:14)

> **Instead of your thoughts being obsessed with dire financial forecasts, unemployment rates, and home foreclosures, focus on God's promise that your rain of blessing is coming and your harvest is ready!**

God says, "I *will* give you the rain, and you *will* gather your grain, your new wine, and your oil." Instead of your thoughts being obsessed with dire financial forecasts, unemployment rates, and home foreclosures, you are focusing on God's promise that your rain of blessing is coming and your harvest is ready!

Reading and praying these Scriptures takes only about ten minutes out of your morning. And, according to the researchers, that's about how much time it takes to turn your day from failure to success, from negative to positive, and from losing to winning. That's what it takes to steer the rudder of your ship from the rocky shores to the still, peaceful waters.

Of course, your prayers don't need to stop there—after all, the apostle Paul told us to *"pray without ceasing"* (1 Thessalonians 5:17)—but this is God's way of pointing you in the right direction, toward His positive, victorious plan for your life.

I remember one morning when Tiz and I were looking for a new building for our church here in Dallas. We had been seeking God in prayer, asking, "Lord, do we build? Should we buy? Lord, what do You have for us?" Only a few days prior, we had looked at a beautiful church that had everything we needed. As I awoke that morning, my very first thoughts were on this new building: *How are we going to do this? What if something goes wrong?*

Immediately, the devil tried to start my day off with negative thoughts. I knew that thoughts of fear and failure do not come from God but from the devil, who *"does not come except to steal, and to kill, and to destroy"* (John 10:10) the dreams and visions God has for my life. So, before I put one foot on the floor to start my day, I set out to defeat the devil through praise. While I was still in bed, I began to praise God. I praised Him for being *Jehovah Jireh*—my Provider. I praised Him for making me more than a conqueror. (See Romans 8:37.) I praised Him because I knew that if He was for me, who could be against me? (See Romans 8:31.) I praised Him for promising that everything I put my hands to, He would cause to prosper. (See Deuteronomy 28:8.) After only a few minutes, instead of stumbling out of bed filled with fear and worry, I charged into my day filled with the Spirit of God.

Then, I read Deuteronomy 6:10–11:

So it shall be, when the Lord your God brings you into the land of which He swore to your fathers, to Abraham, Isaac, and Jacob, to give you large and beautiful cities which you did not build, houses full of all good things, which you did not fill, hewn-out wells which you did not dig, vineyards and olive trees which you did not plant; when you have eaten and are full....

Do you see what God said to me? *"So it shall be."* Large and beautiful cities, houses full of all good things, wells, vineyards, and olive trees for *"when you have eaten and are full."* We serve a God of more than enough, a God of good measure, pressed down and overflowing. I love that. No matter what happens in the news, you and I serve an overflowing God!

Let me share how God provided for the prayers of one man at our church. This man's wife had recently undergone back surgery, and, although she was recovering, she remained out of work. Then, her husband took ill and couldn't work. This left an incredible dent in this family's finances. At one point, they needed one thousand dollars by the end of the week in order to pay the rent. With only a few days left before the rent was due, this man sent us an e-mail asking us to agree with him in prayer for a true miracle of provision from God. In his e-mail, the man said that he remembered the teaching I had done on the *modeh ani*. He recalled that I had cited a study that suggested the first ten minutes of the morning set the course for the rest of the day. He remembered that I had said we were to pray regardless of our circumstances. Since he had picked up a card the church had provided with the *modeh ani* prayers on it, he figured, *What do I have to lose?*

This man was filled with praise and thanksgiving when he reported that just before leaving the house to go to work, he had checked their bank account and found that his payroll deposit was two thousand dollars more than the usual amount. He had received an unexpected bonus! This man was grateful to God and doubly grateful we had taught him that our God is a good God and that His plan for us is to experience His goodness on a daily basis!

The Wisdom of the Rooster

We are to start each day thanking God. In ancient Jewish wisdom, there is a teaching I love about a rooster. The teaching tells us that we are to thank God for giving the rooster understanding to distinguish between day and night. Although most of us don't live with roosters these days, roosters used to be nature's alarm clock. How amazing that God gave man a wake-up call long before the days of clocks and electricity! Why a special prayer concerning a rooster? It's not that hard to tell the difference between light and dark, day and night. But it's not until we understand *when* the rooster actually crows that we understand what God is teaching us.

It would be no great feat if the rooster saw the morning light breaking through the darkness as a signal that he should crow. But that's not what happens. Roosters crow *before* they see the light. They sense that dawn will break soon and that light is on its way to remove the darkness. That's when they begin to crow.

Ancient Jewish wisdom says that a wise person will learn from the rooster. We know that darkness is only temporary, not permanent, and that God's light is always on the way. The rooster is an example of how we should start each day—with a heart full of joy, hope, and faith. The rooster teaches us to see, speak, and celebrate God's blessings even before we actually see them. What a great way to express *modeh ani.*

One of our church members was faithful to always pray the same covering over his daughter that I pray over our church every Sunday. Each day, this man stood in prayer for his daughter. One day, his daughter suffered a seizure and passed out while she was behind the wheel of her car, driving to Oklahoma. That was bad enough, but she had set the cruise control on the car and was traveling around seventy miles per hour. Think about passing out in a car going that fast with no steering or brake control whatsoever. She woke up in the hospital with just a few bruises but no cuts or broken bones. She was sore for a few days, but, other than that, she was in perfect shape. Does God provide a covering to protect our children? Yes! This father knows that, because he daily prayed a covering over his daughter, she was miraculously covered by her heavenly Father.

Each and every morning, we should use God's rudder in order to set the course of our lives in the right direction. It takes only ten minutes. Instead of jumping up, running around, yelling at your kids, and turning on the bad news, start your day in the peace and blessings of God—*modeh ani*—so that it may continue that way until the next day dawns. "Lord, I give You thanks!" should be the first words you speak every morning.

Jesus said, *"I say to you that if two of you agree on earth concerning anything that they ask, it will be done for them by My Father in heaven"* (Matthew 18:19). Your rain is coming. Your harvest is ready. Your house shall be full of *all* good things. You will reap *all* of God's promises. You, your children, and your grandchildren will serve God all of your lives.

In order to help you begin your day with the *modeh ani* in a way that will bless your life and your household, I have included the following simple instructions.

Modeh Ani:
Begin Your Day with Praise and Thanksgiving

The four steps below are to guide you as you begin your day. They are drawn from ancient Judeo-Christian traditions and teachings. Each prayer is listed in both English and phonetic Hebrew. As you follow these steps first thing in the morning, you release the presence, power, and promises of God over you, your family, your health, your finances, and your future. Those first ten minutes have the power to change your destiny forever!

1. Start the morning by praying, "Modeh ani."

I give thanks to You, living and eternal King, for You have restored my soul within me; Your faithfulness is great.

Modeh anee lifanecha melech chai vikayam, she-he-chezarta bee nishmatee b'cherila, raba emunatecha.

Before our feet hit the ground, our first words each morning are "modeh ani"—literally, "I give thanks." This special prayer expresses appreciation to our Father that *"this is the day the LORD has made"* (Psalm 118:24). This prayer lays our foundation for the entire day because we are entering into God's presence with praise and thanksgiving.

2. Wash your hands.

Blessed are You, Lord our God, King of the universe, who has sanctified us with Your commandments and commanded us concerning the washing of the hands.

Baruch atoh Adonoi Eloheinu melech hoolom asher kideshanu bemitzvosov vitzivonu al netilat yadayim.

The *modeh ani* prayer is followed by the washing of the hands, which, in ancient wisdom, is a form of baptism. This ritual is to symbolize being spiritually "born again" so that you may start your day with a new beginning and without any natural limitations. It's this washing with water that renews our minds and breaks any contact with past failures.

3. *Wrap yourself in the tallit.*

Blessed are You, Lord our God, King of the universe, who has sanctified us with Your commandments and commanded us to wrap ourselves with the tallit.

Baruch atoh Adonoy Elohainu melech hoolom asher kidshanu bemitzvosov vitzivonu l'hitatef b'tzitzit.

Once you have prayed the *modeh ani* and washed your hands, you cover yourself in a tallit—a Hebrew prayer shawl—a powerful biblical symbol of faith and prayer. As we discussed in chapter 8, Jesus wore a tallit, which became a point of contact to heal many who were sick. Today, this special garment still plays a significant role in manifesting God's healing power and promises. As you wrap yourself in the tallit, you are entering the secret place of the Most High, your personal Holy of Holies. Here in this place where you hear the voice of God, the enemy is silenced and cannot cause any doubt or confusion.

4. *Speak the* Shema.

Hear, O Israel, the Lord is our God, the Lord is One.

Sh'ma Yis'ra'eil Adonai Eloheinu Adonai echad.

The *Shema* is the daily declaration of faith in Judaism and is recited beneath the tallit. This powerful, unifying statement expresses your loyalty to God, to the Torah, to Israel, and to all the principles, values, and commandments in the Bible. As you say it, it is customary to place your dominant hand above your eyes as a sign of focus and humility. All three Scriptures should be read.

1) Deuteronomy 6:4–9

Hear, O Israel: the Lord our God, the Lord is one! You shall love the Lord your God with all your heart, with all your soul, and with all your strength. And these words which I command you today shall be in your heart. You shall teach them diligently to your children, and shall talk of them when you sit in your house, when you walk by the way, when you lie down, and when you rise up. You shall bind them as a sign on your hand, and they shall be as frontlets between your eyes. You shall write them on the doorposts of your house and on your gates.

2) Deuteronomy 11:13–21

And it shall be that if you earnestly obey My commandments which I command you today, to love the Lord your God and serve Him with all your heart and with all your soul, then I will give you the rain for your land in its season, the early rain and the latter rain, that you may gather in your grain, your new wine, and your oil. And I will send grass in your fields for your livestock, that you may eat and be filled. Take heed to yourselves, lest your heart be deceived, and you turn aside and serve other gods and worship them, lest the Lord's anger be aroused against you, and He shut up the heavens so that there be no rain, and the land yield no produce, and you perish quickly from the good land which the LORD is giving you. Therefore you shall lay up these words of mine in your heart and in your soul, and bind them as a sign on your hand, and they shall be as frontlets between your eyes. You shall teach them to your children, speaking of them when you sit in your house, when you walk by the way, when you lie down, and when you rise up. And you shall write them on the doorposts of your house and on your gates, that your days and the days of your children may be multiplied in the land of which the LORD swore to your fathers to give them, like the days of the heavens above the earth.

3) Numbers 15:37–41

Again the LORD spoke to Moses, saying, "Speak to the children of Israel: Tell them to make tassels on the corners of their garments throughout their generations, and to put a blue thread in the tassels of the corners. And you shall have the tassel, that you may look upon it and remember all the commandments of the LORD and do them, and that you may not follow the harlotry to which your own heart and your own eyes are inclined, and that you may remember and do all My commandments, and be holy for your God. I am the LORD your God, who brought you out of the land of Egypt, to be your God: I am the LORD your God."

Baptism and the Spirit of God

Therefore let all the house of Israel know assuredly that God has made this Jesus, whom you crucified, both Lord and Christ. Now when they heard this, they were cut to the heart, and said to Peter and the rest of the apostles, "Men and brethren, what shall we do?" Then Peter said to them, "Repent, and let every one of you be baptized in the name of Jesus Christ for the remission of sins; and you shall receive the gift of the Holy Spirit. For the promise is to you and to your children, and to all who are afar off, as many as the Lord our God will call." (Acts 2:36–39)

I wanted to begin with this Scripture because it is used frequently in the call to be baptized. As Christians, we know that after we come to God, one of the first things we are to do is be baptized.

To understand what baptism is, we first must understand what it is not. Baptism is not a requirement for joining a church. Baptism is also not a public forum to show the world an outward sign of the inward work of repenting from sin. It is not a way of publicly declaring that you now serve God.

Let's look at the most significant baptism in Scripture:

Then Jesus came from Galilee to John at the Jordan to be baptized by him. And John tried to prevent Him, saying, "I need to be baptized by You, and are You coming to me?" But Jesus answered and said to him, "Permit it to be so now, for thus it is fitting for us to fulfill all righteousness." Then he allowed Him. When He had been baptized, Jesus came up immediately from the water; and behold, the heavens were opened to Him, and He saw the Spirit of God descending like a dove and alighting upon Him. And suddenly a voice came from heaven, saying, "This is My beloved Son, in whom I am well pleased."　　　　(Matthew 3:13–17)

Why did Jesus need to be baptized? It certainly wasn't in order to join some church; Jesus wasn't joining anything. It wasn't an outward sign of an inward work to repent from sin; Jesus *"knew no sin"* (2 Corinthians 5:21). Why, then, did Jesus need to be baptized? For that matter, why do we need to be baptized? The answer may surprise you.

First, we need to understand that baptism didn't start with Christianity.

The baptismal water (*mikveh*) in rabbinic literature was referred to as the womb of the world, and as a convert came out of the water it was considered a new birth separating him from the pagan world. As the convert came out of these waters his status was changed and he was referred to as "a little child just born" or "a child of one day" (Yeb. 22a; 48b; 97b). We see the New Testament using similar Jewish terms as "born anew," "new creation," and "born from above"....[7]

The revered twelfth-century Jewish scholar Maimonides said,

By three things did Israel enter into the Covenant: by circumcision, and baptism and sacrifice....When a Gentile is willing to enter the covenant...he must be

[7]Ron Moseley, Ph.D., "The Jewish Background of Christian Baptism" (originally published in *The Tree of Life* magazine), http://www.bebaptized.org/Jewishroots.htm.

circumcised and be baptized and bring a sacrifice.... The Gentile that is made a proselyte and the slave that is made free, behold he is like a child new born.[8]

You have already been circumcised in your heart. *"He is a Jew who is one inwardly; and circumcision is that of the heart"* (Romans 2:29).

The sacrifice has already been made. *"It is the blood that makes atonement for the soul"* (Leviticus 17:11). *"Without shedding of blood there is no remission"* (Hebrews 9:22).

Now, let's take a closer look at what happens spiritually through biblical baptism. Remember that baptismal water (*mikveh*) was called the "womb of the world...a new birth."

Let's consider this conversation between Jesus and Nicodemus:

Now there was a man of the Pharisees named Nicodemus, a member of the Jewish ruling council. He came to Jesus at night and said, "Rabbi, we know you are a teacher who has come from God. For no one could perform the miraculous signs you are doing if God were not with him." In reply Jesus declared, "I tell you the truth, no one can see the kingdom of God unless he is born again." "How can a man be born when he is old?" Nicodemus asked. "Surely he cannot enter a second time into his mother's womb to be born!" Jesus answered, "I tell you the truth, no one can enter the kingdom of God unless he is born of water and the Spirit." (John 3:1–5 NIV)

Jesus was saying, in effect, "Unless you are born again you cannot 'see'—or understand—the things of the kingdom of God." Then, in verse 10, Jesus said, *"Are you the teacher of Israel, and do not know these things?"* In other words, Nicodemus was a rabbi who taught God's Word. He should have known the

---

[8]Dr. William Wall, *The History of Infant-Baptism*, vol. 1 (New York: Appleton, 1890), 12, 17. See also M. Maimonides, *Issuri Bia,* chaps. 12–14.

answer. As we have seen, to enter into the *mikveh* (the waters of baptism) and come out again is called, in Hebrew, "the womb of the world" and "a new birth." Coming out of the waters of baptism is a powerful, supernatural statement and a big part of spiritual new birth.

> **When we are "born again," not only are we forgiven, but also every curse is broken over our lives. It is a brand-new start.**

Recall Peter's words on the day of Pentecost: *"Repent, and let every one of you be baptized in the name of Jesus Christ for the remission of sins; and you shall receive the gift of the Holy Spirit"* (Acts 2:38). The word *"remission"* is the noun form of "to remit," which means "to release from bondage or imprisonment, forgiveness or pardon, of sins (letting them go as if they had never been committed)." Baptism is powerful. When we are "born again," not only are we forgiven, but also every curse is broken over our lives. It is a brand-new start. Baptism removes the *contract* and the *contact* the enemy has put on your failure.

Jewish wisdom teaches that when we come out of the baptismal waters, failure is removed from our lives. Jesus said to John, in effect, "Baptize Me." When Jesus came out of those waters, the world's limitations were supernaturally removed, the Holy Spirit came upon Him, and His ministry began.

Let me share how baptism produced a similar result in one of our church members. This woman had signed up to go on one of our trips to Israel. The year before, she had been rushed to the hospital with symptoms of what she thought was a heart attack but turned out to be an anxiety attack. Ever since then, she had felt ashamed and embarrassed that something like that could have happened to her while she had been interceding in prayer on behalf of others at our church. She knew that a door had been opened to allow fear to enter her life, yet she didn't know how to get rid of it. In Israel, I was getting ready to baptize people in the Jordan River. We had selected a different location from where we had done baptisms there before. I sensed that this part of the Jordan was more private and more anointed, and I knew that God had something special planned. As we stood on that riverbank, I taught that everyone needed to claim complete deliverance from any and all hindrances that might be operating in his or her life. This woman came forward for baptism, and, as I submerged her, I claimed healing from anxiety, not even knowing what she had been going through!

After she returned home from Israel, she received a call from her doctor, who said that the medical tests she had taken before the trip had revealed something suspicious. At that very moment, she was reminded of when I baptized her in the Jordan River, and, once again, she claimed her complete healing and freedom from anxiety. Then, she went to see her doctor and had more tests done, all of which came back negative—she was free of any and all disease! Afterward, she told us that if she had faced the same situation before our trip to Israel, the outcome would have been different! Through that trip, the Word of God became real to her—specifically, how Jesus had paid the price in full for her complete healing and freedom. She knows that when I baptized her, she received all the healing for which Jesus had already paid the price. Today, she is free, healed, and so full of joy that each time I see her smiling face, it reminds me of God's mighty provision.

Baptism (*mikveh*) brings a spiritual cleansing of the mind and spirit. Rabbis teach that baptism reawakens our spirits, which grow weaker through contact with this world but become alive—reborn—through the water of *mikveh*.

> *But when the kindness and the love of God our Savior toward man appeared, not by works of righteousness which we have done, but according to His mercy He saved us, **through the washing** of regeneration and renewing of the Holy Spirit.*
>
> (Titus 3:4–5, emphasis added)

Jesus and John the Baptist knew what God's Word teaches. At least once a year, during Yom Kippur, every Jew was to be rebaptized, by which God would give them a *"renewing of the Holy Spirit."* We are constantly in contact with spirits of negativity and destruction. This is one of the ways in which God renews and refreshes our spirits and minds.

Several times a year, Tiz and I do a three-day teaching on breaking the curse and releasing the blessing. So many people have gone through battles and are in need of a spiritual "new beginning." After a couple of days of teaching, we always end the weekend with water baptism—a new spiritual birth and a fresh start.

> *For this reason a man shall leave his father and mother and be joined to his wife, and the two shall become one flesh. This is a great mystery, but I speak concerning Christ and the church.* (Ephesians 5:31–32)

This *"great mystery"* was about husbands and wives but also about Christ and the church. What was the connection? Husbands are to love their wives. That's no mystery. Christ loves us. That's no mystery. We need to remember that Paul was a Jew, and he was sharing things that we will miss unless we read them through Jewish eyes. Here's the key:

> *Husbands, love your wives, just as Christ also loved the church and gave Himself for her, that He might **sanctify and cleanse** her with the washing of water by the word.* (verses 25–26, emphasis added)

This was an extremely Jewish understanding of a person's new life with God, or of life between a husband and wife. In her book *The New Jewish Wedding*, author Anita Diamant says,

> All converts to Judaism are required to immerse themselves in the mikvah [sic], marking their rebirth as members of the people of Israel. Some Jews—both men and women—go to mikvah [sic] in preparation

for Yom Kippur, when one has the opportunity to begin the year with a pure heart. According to the Talmud, the ultimate source of all water is the river that emerged from Eden. By immersing themselves in a mikvah [sic], people participate in the wholeness of Eden and are reborn.[9]

The *mikveh* also represents the physical source of life, "the wombs" from which humans enter the world untouched by sin. For brides and grooms, the *mikveh* is the transformation from being single to being married. Entering the *huppah* (wedding canopy) is a public declaration of a change of status; entering the *mikveh* (waters) is a private transformation. Immersion creates newborns—virgins—so *mikveh* can be seen as the demarcation between premarital and married sexuality.

Simply put, our old lives are washed away when we repent and become baptized. God gives us a rebirth, a new spirit. We get to start over again. Because of His great love for us, God will never bring up our pasts. The same goes for husbands and wives who go into the water (*mikveh*) before their marriage. Just as God will never bring up our pasts, we need to love our spouses as much as God loves us and not hold their pasts against them. In fact, when a bride (remember, we, as Christians, are the bride of Christ) comes out of the *mikveh*, no request she makes will be refused. Nothing is allowed to interfere with her happiness.

> **God gives us a rebirth, a new spirit. We get to start over again. Because of His great love for us, God will never bring up our pasts.**

Ancient Jewish wisdom teaches that (1) when you are baptized, you leave this evil world and enter a spiritual world, (2) you break contact with this world of impurity and failure, and (3) you go to a higher level of God consciousness, one in which you can hear His voice more clearly.

---

[9]Anita Diamant, *The New Jewish Wedding* (New York: Fireside, 2001), 150.

Now it happened, as I journeyed and came near Damascus at about noon, suddenly a great light from heaven shone around me. And I fell to the ground and heard a voice saying to me, "Saul, Saul, why are you persecuting Me?" So I answered, "Who are You, Lord?" And He said to me, "I am Jesus of Nazareth, whom you are persecuting." And those who were with me indeed saw the light and were afraid, but they did not hear the voice of Him who spoke to me. So I said, "What shall I do, Lord?" And the Lord said to me, "Arise and go into Damascus, and there you will be told all things which are appointed for you to do." And since I could not see for the glory of that light, being led by the hand of those who were with me, I came into Damascus. Then a certain Ananias, a devout man according to the law, having a good testimony with all the Jews who dwelt there, came to me; and he stood and said to me, "Brother Saul, receive your sight." And at that same hour I looked up at him. Then he said, "The God of our fathers has chosen you that you should know His will, and see the Just One, and hear the voice of His mouth. For you will be His witness to all men of what you have seen and heard. And now why are you waiting? Arise and be baptized, and wash away your sins, calling on the name of the Lord." (Acts 22:6–16)

After his baptism, God spiritually and physically opened Paul's eyes. This is what Jesus told Nicodemus, saying, in effect, "Nicodemus, the *mikveh* baptism is not just a ritual; it is supernatural, and unless you know this, you cannot see the kingdom of God." John the Baptist baptized people to prepare them to see and recognize the Messiah when He came. Peter said, *"You shall receive the gift of the Holy Spirit"* (Acts 2:38). According to ancient Jewish wisdom, to receive the Spirit of God—to be in the presence of the *shekinah*—you must be baptized. God has always used both water and Spirit to bring about rebirth.

Nicodemus said, *"How can a man be born when he is old?...
Surely he cannot enter a second time into his mother's womb to
be born!"* (John 3:4 NIV). Jesus seemed amazed that Nicodemus
didn't know that the *mikveh* was also known as the "womb of
the world." He answered, *"I tell you the truth, no one can enter
the kingdom of God unless he is born of water and the Spirit"*
(verse 5 NIV). We can enter the kingdom of God now by having
our eyes opened and by receiving His Spirit.

Look at a few instances where God used Spirit and water
to bring about new birth.

> *In the beginning God created the heavens and the
> earth. The earth was without form, and void; and
> darkness was on the face of the deep. And the Spirit
> of God was hovering over the face of the waters. Then
> God said, "Let there be light"; and there was light. And
> God saw the light, that it was good; and God divided
> the light from the darkness. God called the light Day,
> and the darkness He called Night. So the evening and
> the morning were the first day.... Then God said, "Let
> the waters under the heavens be gathered together
> into one place, and let the dry land appear"; and it
> was so. And God called the dry land Earth, and the
> gathering together of the waters He called Seas. And
> God saw that it was good.* (Genesis 1:1–5, 9–10)

God brought the world from darkness to light through His
Spirit and the gathering of waters. We also see this when God
delivered the Israelites out of Egypt by parting the Red Sea
(waters). They crossed to the other side, and God's Spirit led
them by day and by night.

When God sent the flood, He put Noah and his family in
the ark, separating them from the waters that inundated the
rest of the world. When God was done, a dove—a symbol of
God's Spirit—brought them word. Remember what happened
when Jesus came out of the Jordan after His baptism: *"And*

John bore witness, saying, 'I saw the Spirit descending from heaven like a dove, and He remained upon Him'" (John 1:32). Eight weeks after Noah saw the dove, God brought him and his family to dry land. Eight is the number that symbolizes new beginnings.

At the wedding feast in Cana, Jesus turned the water into wine.

> *On the third day there was a wedding in Cana of Galilee, and the mother of Jesus was there. Now both Jesus and His disciples were invited to the wedding. And when they ran out of wine, the mother of Jesus said to Him, "They have no wine." Jesus said to her, "Woman, what does your concern have to do with Me? My hour has not yet come." His mother said to the servants, "Whatever He says to you, do it." Now there were set there six waterpots of stone, according to the manner of purification of the Jews, containing twenty or thirty gallons apiece. Jesus said to them, "Fill the waterpots with water." And they filled them up to the brim. And He said to them, "Draw some out now, and take it to the master of the feast." And they took it. When the master of the feast had tasted the water that was made wine, and did not know where it came from (but the servants who had drawn the water knew), the master of the feast called the bridegroom. And he said to him, "Every man at the beginning sets out the good wine, and when the guests have well drunk, then the inferior. You have kept the good wine until now!"*
>
> (John 2:1–10)

Look at what God told Israel through the prophet Ezekiel:

> *For I will take you from among the nations, gather you out of all countries, and bring you into your own land. Then I will sprinkle clean water on you, and you shall be clean; I will cleanse you from all your filthiness and*

*from all your idols. I will give you a new heart and put
a new spirit within you; I will take the heart of stone
out of your flesh and give you a heart of flesh. I will put
My Spirit within you and cause you to walk in My statutes, and you will keep My judgments and do them.
Then you shall dwell in the land that I gave to your
fathers; you shall be My people, and I will be your God.
I will deliver you from all your uncleannesses. I will
call for the grain and multiply it, and bring no famine
upon you. And I will multiply the fruit of your trees
and the increase of your fields, so that you need never
again bear the reproach of famine among the nations.*
(Ezekiel 36:24–30)

In this prophecy, God told the Israelites of a time when there
would be miraculous provision in their lives. He used several
images to convey this: clean water, a new heart, and His Spirit.
When Jesus was on the cross, the soldiers pierced His side, and
blood and water flowed out of the wound. (See John 19:34.)

Being baptized is not just a religious ritual but a supernatural act. According to the historian Josephus, there are six
levels in baptism. The highest level, *mikvaot*, is baptism in the
Jordan River itself. Many believe that the Jordan River is the
same river that flowed from the garden of Eden in Genesis 2:10.
Could this be why Elisha told Naaman to go and wash in the
Jordan seven times in 1 Kings 5:10? Could this be why John
baptized Jesus in the Jordan? No one knows for sure. What I
do know is that when we obey God, the supernatural happens.
There is a rebirth within our spirits.

If you ever find yourself in Israel, why not get baptized
again in the Jordan River? I know that God would fill you with
a fresh anointing of His Spirit.

*For Christ also suffered once for sins, the just for the
unjust, that He might bring us to God, being put to*

death in the flesh but made alive by the Spirit, by whom also He went and preached to the spirits in prison, who formerly were disobedient, when once the Divine longsuffering waited in the days of Noah, while the ark was being prepared, in which a few, that is, eight souls, were saved through water. There is also an antitype which now saves us; baptism (not the removal of the filth of the flesh, but the answer of a good conscience toward God), through the resurrection of Jesus Christ. (1 Peter 3:18–21)

Unveiling the Tabernacle
of David

Without a doubt, one of the greatest signs of prophecy has been the reestablishment of the nation of Israel, along with the return to the Promised Land by Jewish people from around the world. But I couldn't end this book without talking about another incredible prophecy that we are witnessing right now. Amos spoke it, and, as we'll see later, it is also found in the book of Acts.

> *"On that day I will raise up the tabernacle of David, which has fallen down, and repair its damages; I will raise up its ruins, and rebuild it as in the days of old; that they may possess the remnant of Edom, and all the Gentiles who are called by My name," says the* LORD *who does this thing.* (Amos 9:11–12)

In the days of the early church, God sent the apostle Peter to the house of a Roman centurion named Cornelius. At first, this may seem like an insignificant event, but it was about to change the entire world.

> *There was a certain man in Caesarea called Cornelius, a centurion of what was called the Italian Regiment, a devout man and one who feared God with all his household, who gave alms generously to the people,*

and prayed to God always. About the ninth hour of the day he saw clearly in a vision an angel of God coming in and saying to him, "Cornelius!" And when he observed him, he was afraid, and said, "What is it, lord?" So he said to him, "Your prayers and your alms have come up for a memorial before God. Now send men to Joppa, and send for Simon whose surname is Peter." (Acts 10:1–5)

Cornelius was a Gentile, a non-Jew. At this point in time, God had not yet moved through the Gentiles. They were still seen by Jews as unclean, ungodly, and, in the eyes of some, unworthy. After Cornelius saw the angel, he sent men to Joppa to find Peter. At the same time, Peter went to the housetop to pray, where he had a vision of all kinds of unclean, nonkosher animals being set before him and heard a voice telling him to eat them. (See verses 10–13.) When Peter refused, God said, *"What God has cleansed you must not call* [unclean]*"* (verse 15).

The men sent by Cornelius met Peter. Because of his vision, Peter understood that the "unclean" animals he had seen represented the Gentiles of the world. Therefore, Peter went with these men to Caesarea and to Cornelius' house, where he admitted, "In truth I perceive that God shows no partiality" (verse 34). As Peter was declaring this new work of the Lord, God poured out His Spirit and gave the Gentiles the gift of the Holy Spirit.

While Peter was still speaking these words, the Holy Spirit fell upon all those who heard the word. And those of the circumcision who believed were astonished, as many as came with Peter, because the gift of the Holy Spirit had been poured out on the Gentiles also. For they heard them speak with tongues and magnify God. (verses 44–46)

Eventually, a dispute arose as to how the Gentiles were to be incorporated into the synagogues and whether or not they needed to be circumcised. When a council of apostles and elders was convened in Jerusalem to consider these issues, Paul and Barnabas testified before them.

> Then all the multitude kept silent and listened to Barnabas and Paul declaring how many miracles and wonders God had worked through them among the Gentiles. (Acts 15:12)

Then, the apostle James addressed the council by reminding them of the words of the prophet Amos.

> And after they had become silent, James answered, saying, "Men and brethren, listen to me: Simon has declared how God at the first visited the Gentiles to take out of them a people for His name. And with this the words of the prophets agree, just as it is written: 'After this I will return and will rebuild the tabernacle of David, which has fallen down; I will rebuild its ruins, and I will set it up; so that the rest of mankind may seek the LORD, even all the Gentiles who are called by My name, says the LORD who does all these things.'"
>
> (verses 13–17)

In this passage, James said, "Simon has declared how God at the first visited the Gentiles to take out of them a people for His name. And with this the words of the prophets **agree**" (emphasis added). The Greek word translated as "agree" means "to be in accord, to harmonize." Like the voices in a choir or instruments in an orchestra, they are all in harmony together on this issue. James suggested that this harmony was the prophetic sign to "rebuild the tabernacle of David."

To explain what the tabernacle of David was, it might be best to establish what it wasn't, or isn't. It is not a reference to Solomon's temple. This is an important distinction! Amos 1:1 says, "The words of Amos...which he saw concerning Israel in the days of Uzziah king of Judah." When Uzziah was the king of Judah, the temple of Solomon was still standing in all its glory and splendor. Its services and sacrifices were all fully functional. So, while Solomon's temple was still standing, God declared through His prophet Amos that His purpose was to raise up, once again, *"the tabernacle of David"* (Amos 9:11).

Look again at the full passage:

"On that day I will raise up the tabernacle of David, which has fallen down, and repair its damages; I will raise up its ruins, and rebuild it as in the days of old; that they may possess the remnant of Edom, and all the Gentiles who are called by My name," says the LORD *who does this thing.* (verses 11–12)

God said He would *"raise up the tabernacle of David, which has fallen down, and repair its damages."* Historically, the tabernacle of David wasn't a building but a tent that housed the ark of the covenant, which represented the presence of God on earth.

Now it was told King David, saying, "The LORD *has blessed the house of Obed-Edom and all that belongs to him, because of the ark of God." So David went and brought up the ark of God from the house of Obed-Edom to the City of David with gladness....So they brought the ark of the* LORD, *and set it in its place in the midst of the tabernacle that David had erected for it. Then David offered burnt offerings and peace offerings before the* LORD. (2 Samuel 6:12, 17)

At the time of the tabernacle of David, the tabernacle of Moses was still in place at Gibeon, still fully functional with its priests, sacrifices, and other rituals. However, the ark of the covenant was not there. It had been captured by the Philistines. David took back the ark, but instead of taking it to Gideon and putting it in the tabernacle of Moses, he followed God's instruction to take it to Zion and erect a new tabernacle. So, when Amos and James were talking about the rebuilding of the tabernacle of David, they weren't talking about a physical house of

God but a spiritual house of God. We see a prophetic sign that this was about to happen in Acts 15 with the Gentiles' inclusion in the early church, and it's also what we're seeing now in the last church—the wall between Jews and Gentiles coming down.

In the tabernacle of David, there were three miracles taking place. First, and most important, there was no veil or curtain between God and man. God walked among His people with signs, wonders, and miracles. The power and anointing of God was a daily, 24-7 occurrence. When Jesus, the Messiah, comes back to Jerusalem, God will establish His kingdom forever. There will be no more sickness, poverty, or wars. There will be peace in Jerusalem, as well as throughout the entire earth. But before God builds His physical tabernacle of David, He will first rebuild His spiritual tabernacle of David. Some Christians call this the "latter rain," a time when God will manifest with signs and wonders, every moment of every day. How will this happen? It will happen in the last days just as it did in David's day and in the days of Acts.

Here's how it will happen: when David built the tabernacle on Mount Zion, God told him two important things. First, God no longer wanted blood sacrifices but instead sacrifices of praise.

> *Then David spoke to the leaders of the Levites to appoint their brethren to be the singers accompanied by instruments of music, stringed instruments, harps, and cymbals, by raising the voice with resounding joy.* (1 Chronicles 15:16)

Many, if not most, of the psalms were originally prophetic songs given to David in his tabernacle.

The second thing God told David was to make sure there was no wall between the Jews and Gentiles who wanted to serve the God of Abraham, Isaac, and Jacob. God said, in effect, "When I see that no wall is allowed to divide, I will also not allow any wall to stand that keeps you from Me."

Look again at the story of Peter and Cornelius in Acts 10:1–2: *"There was a certain man in Caesarea called Cornelius,…a devout man and one who feared God with all his household, who gave alms generously to the people, and prayed to God always."* This was the beginning of God pouring out His Spirit. Jew and Gentile were coming together.

Now, it's happening again. In the first church, the Jews tore down the wall of separation. In the last church, it's up to you and me to tear down that wall. Here's how.

> *Therefore remember that you, once Gentiles in the flesh; who are called Uncircumcision by what is called the Circumcision made in the flesh by hands; that at that time you were without Christ, being aliens from the commonwealth of Israel and strangers from the covenants of promise, having no hope and without God in the world. But now in Christ Jesus you who once were far off have been brought near by the blood of Christ.* (Ephesians 2:11–13)

The apostle Paul told us that we were *once* Gentiles—*once*, but not anymore.

> *Now, therefore, you are no longer strangers and foreigners, but fellow citizens with the saints and members of the household of God.* (verse 19)

According to Paul, we are *"no longer strangers or foreigners, but **fellow** citizens and members of the household of God."*

Sometimes, we need to be reminded of what Paul said in Romans 11:

> *For if the firstfruit is holy, the lump is also holy; and if the root is holy, so are the branches. And if some of the branches were broken off, and you, being a wild olive tree, were grafted in among them, and with them became a partaker of the root and fatness of the olive tree, do not boast against the branches. But if you do*

boast, remember that you do not support the root, but the root supports you. (Romans 11:16–18)

The firstfruit—Israel—is holy. We Gentiles were grafted in. Yet we have been warned not to boast. We must remember that we—the church, the branches that have been grafted in—do not support the root (the Jews, or Israel), but it is the root that supports us.

For He Himself is our peace, who has made both one, and has broken down the middle wall of separation, having abolished in His flesh the enmity, that is, the law of commandments contained in ordinances, so as to create in Himself one new man from the two, thus making peace. (Ephesians 2:14–15)

Here is the same prophecy God gave Amos during the time of Solomon's temple. It's the same prophecy God spoke through Peter, James, Paul, and Barnabas in the early church. And now, in these last days, God is saying, "As good as it's been, I've got something better." When we tear down the middle wall—the wall that separates Jew and Gentile—God will again pour out His Spirit. He will again come from behind the veil and supernaturally walk among His people. This is what the apostle Paul meant when he said God would *"create in Himself one new man from the two, thus making peace."* The Hebrew word for "peace" is *shalom,* which means there is nothing missing or broken.

> **When we tear down the middle wall—the wall that separates Jew and Gentile—God will again pour out His Spirit. He will again come from behind the veil and supernaturally walk among His people.**

That's why I wrote this book. That's why God has you reading it.

Here is a Scripture that refers to what is called the "fivefold ministry":

*And He Himself gave some to be **apostles**, some **prophets**, some **evangelists**, and some **pastors** and **teachers**, for the equipping of the saints for the work of ministry, for the edifying of the body of Christ, till we all come to the unity of the faith and of the knowledge of the Son of God, to a perfect man, to the measure of the stature of the fullness of Christ.*

(Ephesians 4:11–13, emphasis added)

> **In these last days, you and I are called by the voice of God to be the "tabernacle of David."**

Why does God still employ the five-fold ministry on the earth today? Do we still need apostles and prophets? Do we still need evangelists, pastors, and teachers? The answer is yes. In fact, as we get closer to the end times, we need them more than ever before. God is opening the eyes of Christians to their Jewish roots. As Paul implied in verse 13, to our faith we need to add a knowledge of the Torah, as well as a knowledge of a Jewish man named Moses, a Jewish man named Paul, a Jewish man named Peter, and a Jewish man named Jesus.

This I say, therefore, and testify in the Lord, that you should no longer walk as the rest of the Gentiles walk, in the futility of their mind, having their understanding darkened, being alienated from the life of God, because of the ignorance that is in them, because of the blindness of their heart. (verses 17–18)

According to Paul, once our eyes have been opened, and once we tear down the wall that divides Jew and Gentile, we will no longer walk in darkness, being separated from the life (*l'chaim*) of God. In these last days, you and I are called by the voice of God to be the "tabernacle of David."

You also, as living stones, are being built up a spiritual house, a holy priesthood, to offer up spiritual sacrifices acceptable to God through Jesus Christ. Therefore it is also contained in the Scripture, "Behold, I lay in Zion a chief cornerstone, elect, precious, and he who believes on Him will by no means be put to shame."

(1 Peter 2:5–6)

"Repairer of the Breach"

As the world is seeing the prophetic signs of the return of the Lord, there is an important event that is also coming to pass. Isaiah 58:9–12 prophesies about a *"repairer of the breach."*

Then you shall call, and the LORD will answer; you shall cry, and He will say, "Here I am." If you take away the yoke from your midst, the pointing of the finger, and speaking wickedness, if you extend your soul to the hungry and satisfy the afflicted soul, then your light shall dawn in the darkness, and your darkness shall be as the noonday. The LORD will guide you continually, and satisfy your soul in drought, and strengthen your bones; you shall be like a watered garden, and like a spring of water, whose waters do not fail. Those from among you shall build the old waste places; you shall raise up the foundations of many generations; and you shall be called the Repairer of the Breach, The Restorer of Streets to Dwell In.

This is the repairing of the breach, the tearing down of the walls that divide God's people.

Living Stones

We are "living stones"—stones full of the life of God; stones of joy and peace, of health and prosperity, and of a life that will spiritually build the tabernacle of David so that, one day, God the Father will say, "My children have had their eyes opened, and I have unveiled My secrets to them. Look at them! They are now the head and not the tail. They are as I always intended them to be, lenders and not borrowers. They are above only and not beneath. I have opened the windows of heaven to them, and the entire world now calls them blessed."

The "children of miracles" will be so blessed that the world will run back to God. My prayer for you is that this book will be a tool that God uses to bring you a little more knowledge, and that, in these last days, you will become one of God's "children of miracles."

> *How that by revelation He made known to me the mystery (as I have briefly written already, by which, when you read, you may understand my knowledge in the mystery of Christ), which in other ages was not made known to the sons of men, as it has now been revealed by the Spirit to His holy apostles and prophets: that the Gentiles should be fellow heirs, of the same body, and partakers of His promise in Christ through the gospel.* (Ephesians 3:3–6)

> *And to make all see what is the fellowship of the mystery, which from the beginning of the ages has been hidden in God who created all things through Jesus Christ; to the intent that now the manifold wisdom of God might be made known by the church to the principalities and powers in the heavenly places.*
>
> (verses 9–10)

> *And if you are Christ's, then you are Abraham's seed, and heirs according to the promise!* (Galatians 3:29)

Appendix:
The Firstfruits Offerings

Three times a year [you] *shall appear before the* LORD *your God in the place which He chooses: at the Feast of Unleavened Bread, at the Feast of Weeks, and at the Feast of Tabernacles; and* [you] *shall not appear before the* LORD *empty-handed.*   (Deuteronomy 16:16)

Anytime we give to God, He will bless us. But these offerings are different. These times are special. Each of these offerings produces a particular harvest, or blessing, that is released from heaven to cover you and your family for the entire year. When we seize these special times, Jesus stops and opens the windows of heaven, saying, in effect, "Receive your blessing. Your faith has saved you."

We are to bring special offerings—"firstfruits offerings"—to make sure the windows of heaven do not pass us by. These are offerings above and beyond our tithes that can be given to our own churches, or to any church or ministry that celebrates the Jewish roots of our Christian faith.

Offering	Provides	Bible Reference	Dates
Passover Offering During the second day of Passover, the Feast of Unleavened Bread	Divine grace, favor, and protection from fellow man	Deuteronomy 16:16 Leviticus 23:4–8	Sundown 4/7/2012 3/26/2013 4/15/2014 4/4/2015

Offering	Provides	Bible Reference	Dates
Pentecost Offering Fifty days after Passover (also called Shavuot or the Feast of Weeks)	God's financial favor, help, and equipping	Deuteronomy 16:16 Leviticus 23:15–25	Sundown 5/26/2012 5/14/2013 6/3/2014 5/23/2015
Sukkot Offering (also called the Feast of Tabernacles)	The promise that our harvests will root deeply and produce an abundance of fruit	Deuteronomy 16:16 Leviticus 23:33–43	Sundown 10/12–19/2011 9/31–10/7/2012 9/18–25/2013 10/8–15/2014

Glossary of Terms

Aliyah

Specifically, it is to ascend, or rise. Traditionally used to refer to the return of the Jews to the land of Israel. Also, in the synagogue, it is used to describe the one who is given the great honor of reading the Torah.

El Shaddai

One of the Judaic names of God, commonly translated as "God Almighty" or "the God of more than enough."

Gentile

Any non-Jewish person. Also can refer to a stranger or foreigner.

Jehovah Jireh

In Hebrew, "the Lord will provide." Designation for God, but also refers to the place where Abraham offered to sacrifice his son, Isaac, before God provided a ram to be sacrificed in his place.

Logos

Greek word for "the written word." Also part of the root word by which we derive the English word *logic*.

Mezuzah

A small plaque or parchment applied to the doorway of every Jewish home and containing words from the *Shema*. Fulfills a *mitzvah* from God in Deuteronomy 6:9.

Mikveh

Water used for baptism in Judaism that brings a spiritual cleansing of the mind and spirit.

Mitzvah

Hebrew for "commandment." Refers to the commandments given to us by God. Not just the Ten Commandments, however, but all 613 mitzvahs found in Scripture.

Modeh Ani	Hebrew for "I acknowledge" or "I give thanks." A Jewish prayer said daily upon waking while still in bed.
Passover	In Hebrew, *Pesach*, a yearly Jewish feast, or holy day, recalling Israel's exodus from Egypt and deliverance from slavery. Literally refers to the plague God sent Pharaoh that killed all the firstborn male offspring of Egypt. The application of lamb's blood on the doorposts of Israelite homes caused the curse to "pass over" all within the households.
Pesach	See "Passover."
Rabbi	Hebrew word meaning "great" or "revered," usually referring to a Jewish man who is a teacher of the Torah. Not an occupation but a title.
Rhema	Greek term for the Word of God made alive by the inspiration of the Holy Spirit.
Rosh Hashanah	Hebrew for "head of the year." First day of the Jewish calendar and a ten-day period of reflection and repentance leading to Yom Kippur, the Day of Atonement.
Sabbath	*Shabbat* in Hebrew, a day of rest on the seventh day beginning at sundown every Friday.
Seder	Hebrew word for "order" or "arrangement," but also referring to the meal and ceremony on the first and second nights of Passover.
Shabbat	See "Sabbath."
Shavuot	Hebrew for "weeks." Denotes the Feast of Pentecost, or the Feast of Weeks, celebrating when God gave Moses the first five books of the Old Testament on Mount Sinai.

Shema	Hebrew word for "hear." First word of the daily Jewish prayer that says, "Hear, O Israel: the Lord is our God, the Lord is One." (See Deuteronomy 6:4.)
Sukkot	Hebrew word, plural for "booth" or "hut." Signifies the Feast of Tabernacles, celebrated for seven days after Yom Kippur. A reminder of when Israel lived in the wilderness in makeshift tents, and later worshipped in a portable tabernacle, a forerunner to a permanent temple.
Tallit	A prayer shawl traditionally worn as an outer garment by Jewish men. Edge of the tallit has tassels made with blue thread at the four corners, or wings.
Teshuvah	A Jewish concept that involves returning to God through repentance. Also refers to the forty days leading up to Yom Kippur, the Day of Atonement.
Torah	Hebrew word for "leaning," "instruction," or "law." God's Word or law as a pathway to relationship with our Father. Also refers to the first five books of the Old Testament.
Tzedakah	Hebrew word commonly translated as "charity," but also part of the root word of "justice." Used to refer to acts of kindness.
Yom Kippur	Hebrew for the Day of Atonement. The most solemn of Jewish holidays. During temple worship, it was the day the high priest went into the Holy of Holies to offer a sacrifice that would atone for the sins of the nation for another year.

About the Author

Larry Huch is the founder and senior pastor of DFW New Beginnings in Irving, Texas. Founded in November 2004, this nondenominational church has quickly developed into a diverse, multiethnic congregation of several thousand people. Pastor Larry and his wife, Tiz, are driven by a passionate commitment to see people succeed in every area of life. That passion, along with their enthusiasm, genuine love for people, and effective teaching, has fueled a ministry that spans over thirty years and two continents.

That same energy and commitment to sharing a positive, life-changing, and biblically based message with the world is the hallmark of Pastor Larry's international television program, *New Beginnings*. This program is broadcast weekly to millions of homes around the globe and has served to touch and change the lives of countless people.

Pastor Larry's signature combination of humor, a dynamic teaching style, and a deep understanding of the Bible have made him a much-sought-after guest on television programs, at conferences, and on various other forms of media. Pastor Larry is a pioneer in the area of breaking family curses and has been recognized the world over for his teachings on the subject, along with his best-selling book, *Free at Last*. His follow-up books, *10 Curses That Block the Blessing* and *The Torah Blessing*, are also best sellers. As a successful author, Pastor Larry has been honored by the testimonies of thousands upon thousands of people whose lives have been impacted and forever altered by his testimony and teachings.

Pastor Larry is wholeheartedly committed to bridging the gap between Christians and Jews and restoring the church to its Judeo-Christian roots. He firmly believes in studying, understanding, and teaching the Word from a Jewish perspective. Larry was honored to have spoken at the Israeli Knesset and has received awards from the Knesset Social Welfare Lobby for his ministry's generosity toward the needs of the Jewish people in Israel.

Pastors Larry and Tiz are the proud parents of three wonderful children (and a son-in-law and daughter-in-law), all who are active in ministry. Their three grandchildren, the "sugars," are the loves of their lives!